# The New "Discovery" Technique

## for Art Instruction:

## An Innovative Handbook

## for the Elementary Teacher

Billie M. Phillips

Virginia Suggs Brown

WITHDRAWN

# The New "Discovery" Technique for Art Instruction: An Innovative Handbook for the Elementary Teacher

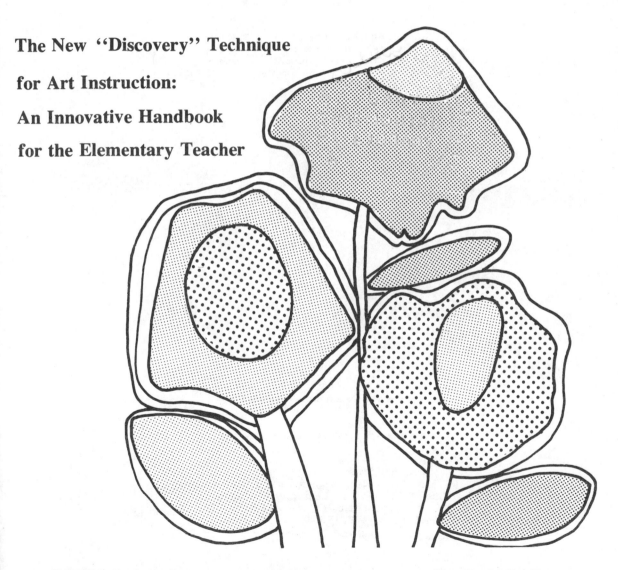

Parker Publishing Company, Inc.        West Nyack, New York

© 1976 by

**Parker Publishing Company, Inc.**
**West Nyack, New York**

**Library of Congress Cataloging in Publication Data**

Phillips, Billie.
   The new "discovery" technique for art instruc-
tion.

   Includes index.
   1.  Art--Study and teaching (Elementary)--U-
nited States.  2.  Learning by discovery.
I.  Brown, Virginia, joint author.  II.  Title.
N353.P44    372.5'044     76-6912
ISBN 0-13-612507-7

Printed in the United States of America

# INTRODUCTION

As a teacher, you look for new and effective ways to introduce your children to new learning experiences. An innovative approach to achieving this goal in art is the use of observation techniques that lead to discovery. The art lessons in this book will enable children to observe colors, and to discover, for example, that under certain conditions a color may appear bright or dull; it may seem far away or very close; or the color may appear to vibrate or recede; to feel warm or cool. The children will then use these observations to progress through succeeding steps of a project. *"Discovery observation" as part of elementary art education is a new idea, an idea which raises your classroom art lesson from merely a pleasant break in the day's routine to an aesthetic project, or more appropriately, an aesthetic experience.*

Another new approach you will find in this book is the active use of prints or reproductions of the works of master artists like Paul Klee, Winslow Homer, Paul Cezanne, Paul Gauguin, and Edgar Degas. You will see how to use these prints to set the stage for your lesson and to focus your children's attention upon effects of particular techniques used successfully in these compositions. You will see how to use these reproductions of masterpieces for lesson follow-up and enrichment. Your children will be challenged to observe, to see, to notice, and to become aware of effects created not only in the artists' works, but also in their own compositions. And you will be providing a forum for your children's free verbal and artistic expression of what they see, feel and think.

You will want to watch for the use of planning as an innovative technique that becomes a natural step in the production of a satisfying and successful project. Your children will sketch ideas or experiment with an arrangement, observe their results, and try the drawings again or change the arrangement if necessary to capture the ideas they had in mind. And then they will use these plans for reference as they produce their works of art.

The "continuing experience" is yet another new idea in this book. In Chapter 1, for example, the children will deal with basic colors and you will extend this experience in Chapters 2 and 3 as your children observe and experiment with certain color characteristics like warmth, coolness, value, and intensity. Then in projects of Chapters 5 and 8, for example, there are opportunities for your children to make practical applications of what they have learned about colors.

Chapter 4 is designed to help your children develop a lasting awareness of the importance and power of the line. In Chapter 5 the children will rediscover the line as they consider and experiment with pattern in repetition. Their growing knowledge about line, pattern, and color will be applied in Chapter 6 where compositions depend upon the circle, square, triangle, and their alterations. From these basic shapes, your children will produce creative lettering, which takes on a new dimension as an artistic and aesthetic experience in Chapter 7.

Medium is the means and discovery is the process in the next chapter. The children's experimentations in Chapter 8 will be with various mixed media including pencil, ink, chalk, crayon, tempera, and cloth textures.

Every chapter opens with a brief introduction of objectives. Next is the section "Before You Begin" that is intended to help you capture your children's interest, spark their thinking about ideas or techniques, and create an atmosphere for the activities that follow for each grade level. You will be easily able to adapt and expand the motivational ideas in this section for classes from kindergarten through sixth grade, since motivation and creativity transcend grade and age barriers. In the major portion of each chapter, there are three groups of practical lessons with accompanying illustrations of various steps and stages. Each group of lessons provides projects with stated goals for Levels K-2, 3-4, and 5-6. After you have used a lesson for your particular grade level, don't feel restricted to only that level. Move up or down to the next grade designation if you think your children are ready for the challenges there. Even if you work with younger children, you may want to try the projects of Chapter 3, which are otherwise suggested only for levels 3-4 and 5-6 because of the medium used.

"Can You Imagine," a series of brief optional activities, completes each lesson. These easy-to-implement activities suggest new and different approaches for strengthening and reinforcing the experiences, techniques, and ideas of a project. Also, the activities are designed to challenge you and your children to think of other applications and variations.

All the art lessons are practical and easy to carry out, with helpful hints appearing the moment you need them. One practical aspect of the lessons in which reproductions, excerpts from literature, and poetry are recommended is that you can readily make substitutions for these suggested selections if you feel the substitutions illustrate the particular techniques and ideas emphasized in the lesson. Another practical aspect is that you may, if necessary, implement each lesson without using the reproductions of artists' works, using films and pictures from other sources.

One approach to using this book as a "how to" or a "project" resource is to glance at the chapter titles and openings to discover what the emphases are, and then simply pick and choose any lessons that seem to fit your various art needs. It is the authors' hope, however, that you will want to start at the beginning of this volume and continue through each chapter in sequence, providing for your children the developmental art experiences that foster learning and creative expression while you yourself are enjoying the success of your teaching effort and the fruits of your children's experimentations. It is the authors' hope that, in turn, the children will be able to translate words like *rage, joy* and *embarrassment* into different values of red; to see a series of rectangles grouped together before they see the telephone booth the rectangles form; to imagine in color; to become curious about works of art; to see the shapes of openings, spaces, and apertures; to reflect upon pattern, design, shape, or texture in buildings and nature; to notice the most subtle color changes around them; and as a result to appreciate and enjoy the broad, exciting world of creativity and to want to participate in it.

*Billie M. Phillips*
*Virginia Suggs Brown*

# Table of Contents

## Chapter 1

**Primary and Secondary Colors - 11**

## Chapter 2

**Warm and Cool Colors - 40**

## Chapter 3

**Value and Intensity - 75**

## Chapter 4

**Line Experiments - 106**

# CHAPTER 1

# PRIMARY AND SECONDARY COLORS

People seem to be conditioned to their own private, little world of color that is undergoing continuous change because of personal involvement with the physical surroundings which directly affect them.

For example, children in Nevada, Utah, or Wyoming normally would grasp the meaning of "earth colors" when shown Andrew Wyeth's painting of open fields. They would have seen the browns tinged with oranges, yellows, and grays; and would have "lived" these earth colors. Children in California would understand the full meaning of a blue sky and the many green hues of nature. Yet, they may not be able to imagine as easily the many gray hues that are a part of the stormy, wintery skies of the middle west. Nor could the expression "as white as snow crystals" have great visual meaning to children in Florida.

Color association and choice and use of color are affected by personal experiences. If experiences are multitudinous and varied, and generally they are, then a person may associate a color with experiences that are often extreme or polarized. A person may associate the primary color *red* with danger, blood, or tragedy; with thoughts of love and affection symbolized by the red heart on a valentine; or with circus scenes and giant balloons.

A person may associate the primary color *blue* with a summer sky, spiritual tranquility, or the quietness of night; with loneliness, coldness, or a mysterious setting.

*Orange*, a secondary color, may suggest a delicious fruit, the warm glow of a fireplace, summer sunrise, agitation, brash noises, or a warm relationship.

*Green*, a secondary color, could bring to mind a cool feeling on a hot day, a seasonal time of the year, or peacefulness. On the other hand, a person might think of "green with envy," a "sick green," or a "green horn."

This chapter contains color experiments that will appeal to children's emotions and help them discover color, develop color awareness, and begin to use color creatively with greater confidence.

## BEFORE YOU BEGIN

Let's begin to think and speak color. Ask the children to close their eyes for the following experiences:

Try to picture a yellow day, a gray day, a rosy afternoon. Which day would seem the warmest? Which day might be the coldest? What might happen on each day? How would you feel on each day?

Picture the sky just before night. What color is the sky? Try to see the brilliant, blinding, powerful colors in a sunrise. How do the colors make you feel?

Picture grass at night. What color does the grass appear to be? Green, gray, or no color?

Try to see a rainbow. Describe your rainbow. How does it make you feel?

Picture a brick building at sunset. What color do red bricks appear to be when the sun is setting?

Try to see street lights coming on at dusk. What color are leaves and other plant life at dusk?

Picture the reflection of trees in a puddle of water on the sidewalk at night with the street light supplying the light. What color is the reflection in the water?

Picture the color yellow on a rainy day. Does the yellow appear to be cheery or dull?

Try to see the mixture of colors in umbrellas carried by people hurrying to work in the rain. What colors do you see? How do they make you feel?

Picture a yellow house far away upon a hill. Picture an orange house on the same hill. Which color house can you see better?

Now that the children have thought and spoken *color*, it is time to experiment with it.

**To begin:**  If you have powdered paint, fill a can of red tempera almost to the top with water. Stir or shake well, until the mixed paint has the smooth consistency of mustard. If you are using liquid tempera, stir the paint well. Children may take turns helping to stir the mixture. In like manner prepare yellow and blue tempera paint.

Have the children name the red, yellow, and blue paints. Indicate that these are the *primary colors* and all other colors can be mixed from these three.

Pour half of the red tempera paint into a jar. Add half of the yellow and mix well. Have children name the new color. Use this procedure for mixing yellow and blue to make green and blue and red to make violet.

Cover the children's desks with newspaper. Give each child a cardboard 9″ × 12″ and a 5″ manila drawing paper circle folded into 6 equal parts (Figure 1-1). Put about 3 tablespoons (1 tablespoon in different spots to represent paint cakes) of each of the red, yellow, and blue mixed tempera on the cardboard. Be sure to leave space between the ''cakes'' of colors. (See Figure 1-2.) *Note:* The 9″ × 12″ cardboard is used as a palette in these experiments and many others throughout the book.

Provide the following directions for the children to experiment with creating a primary and secondary *color wheel*.

- With a 2″ × 4″ cardboard strip, scoop up a small amount of red paint from the

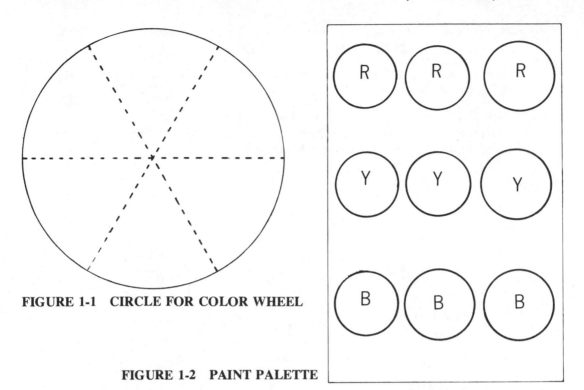

**FIGURE 1-1   CIRCLE FOR COLOR WHEEL**

**FIGURE 1-2   PAINT PALETTE**

palette and spread the paint on one of the spaces of the paper circle. (See Figure 1-3A.) Place the used strip aside on the newspaper. *Note:* The cardboard strip is used as a paintbrush in this experiment and other projects throughout the book.

- Use a clean strip and scoop up a small amount of yellow paint from the palette.

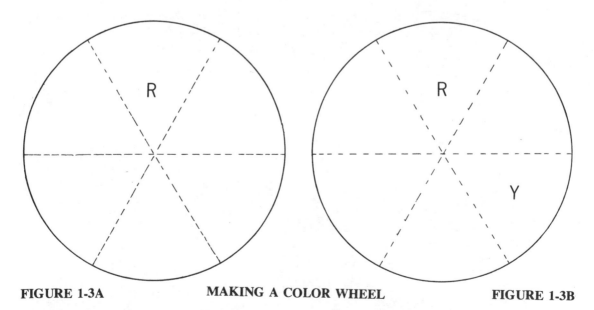

**FIGURE 1-3A**          **MAKING A COLOR WHEEL**          **FIGURE 1-3B**

Skip the space next to the red painted space and paint the third wedge with the yellow paint. (See Figure 1-3B.)

- Using a clean strip, scoop up enough blue paint from the palette to cover the fifth space. (Figure 1-3C.)

- Scoop up a "cake" (spot) of yellow from the palette and mix it with a "cake" of red on the palette. Identify the new color and paint the space orange between the red and yellow on the color wheel. (See Figure 1-3D.)

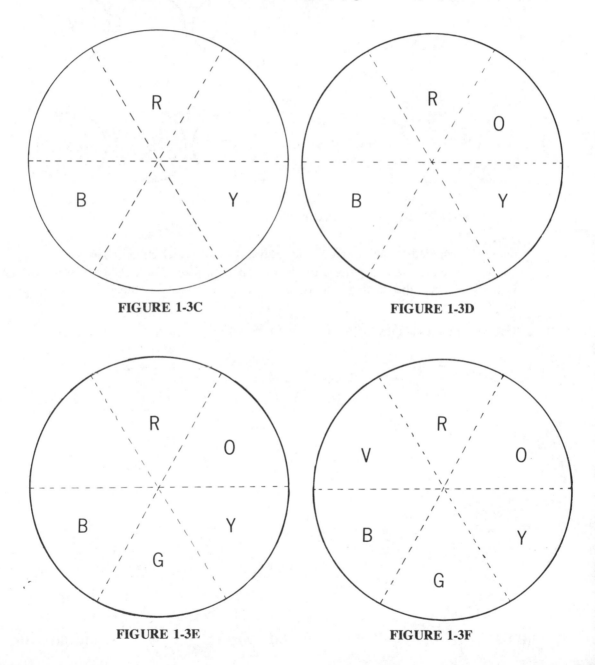

FIGURE 1-3C                            FIGURE 1-3D

FIGURE 1-3E                            FIGURE 1-3F

- Scoop up a "cake" of blue and mix it with one "cake" of yellow on the palette. Identify the new color and paint the space green between the yellow and blue on the color wheel. (See Figure 1-3E.)

- Using a clean strip, scoop up a small amount of blue and mix it with a "cake" of red on the palette. Identify the new color and paint the space violet between the blue and red. (See Figure 1-3F.)

Display magazine pictures and prints of paintings that have dominant primary and secondary colors. Explain that these pictures and paintings are often called *compositions*. A *composition* is an arrangement of line, shape, color and texture within a given area. Have the children study the compositions and identify which one or ones are predominantly red, yellow, blue, orange, green, or violet.

Provide opportunities for children to use the mixed secondary colors in independent or free-choice painting activities.

Preserve several color wheels to use as reference required for projects in Chapter 2.

*Note:* In the "You'll Need" sections throughout the book, the materials are listed for each project. Each child will need one of each item unless otherwise specified, for example, cardboard strips (9 per child). Items for demonstration only or for use by the entire group are preceded by a specific number such as 6 containers or 1 cup. Of course, only one print or reproduction of any painting suggested will be needed.

## SEEING REDS, YELLOWS, AND BLUES (GRADES K-2)

To experiment with variations of the primary colors:

*You'll Need . . .*

Manila drawing paper 12″ × 12″ (3 sheets per child) ● red, blue, and yellow crayons ● index cards 3″ × 5″.

*Procedures . . .*

- On the drawing paper squares, with red crayons the children trace around an index card.
- Make several overlapping tracings of the index card. (Illustration 1-1A.) *Note:* Some children may want to make only five or six tracings. Others may cover their papers with tracings.
- Trace over all lines with the red crayons to make them heavy.
- With the red crayon, children color a different red in each area on the manila square as suggested in Illustration 1-1B. *Note:* On a sheet of paper, demonstrate how light, medium, and dark reds may be achieved by varying the pressure applied to the crayon.
- Use the same procedures to make a composition of yellow variations and a composition of blue variations.

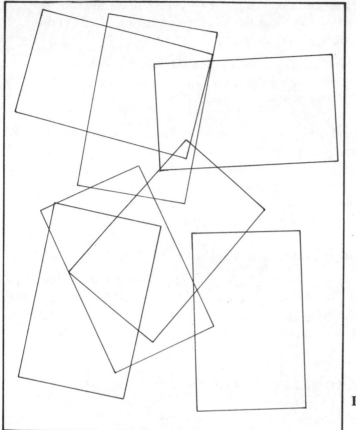

**ILLUSTRATION 1-1A**
**SEEING REDS**

*Can You Imagine . . .*

Create a patch door by covering it with overlapping cloth and paper samples of red, yellow, or blue.

Paste a swatch of cloth on a shirt board or cardboard. Around it paste small squares of the construction paper of the same color of the cloth or of one of the colors if the cloth is multi-colored.

Have a discussion on the dominant color and the items of that color in the following prints that contain red, yellow, or blue: Henry Matisse's *The Red Studio* (red dominance), Van Gogh's *Sunflowers* (yellow), Currier and Ives' *Home to Thanksgiving* (blue dominance).

## THE PRIMARY SQUARES (GRADES 3-4)

To use the primary colors in experiments with blue on blue, red on red, and yellow on yellow designs.

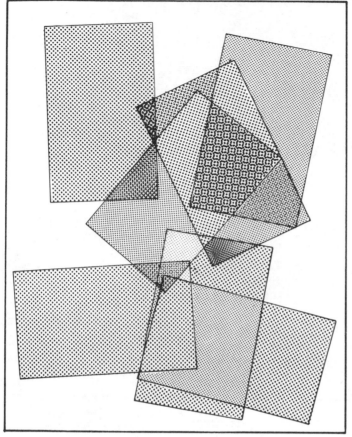

**ILLUSTRATION 1-1B**

*You'll Need . . .*

Drawing paper squares 6″ folded into 16 parts (3 squares per child) ● red, yellow, blue crayons ● paste ● paste dabbers or brushes ● yellow, red, blue, and white construction paper 9″ × 24″ (1 piece per child so that some children will have yellow, some will have red, and so on).

*Procedures . . .*

- On one of the folded squares, color each of the sixteen spaces with the red and blue crayons. *Note:* Red may appear next to red and blue next to blue. (See Illustration 1-2A.) Encourage children to make adjoining spaces of the same color different shades by varying the pressure applied to the crayon. Try to discourage the ordinary checkerboard arrangement.
- On the same square create blue designs on blue spaces and red designs on red spaces. *Note:* Dots, stripes, stars, checks, and other forms of patterns may be used. (See Illustration 1-2B.) All spaces need not contain designs.

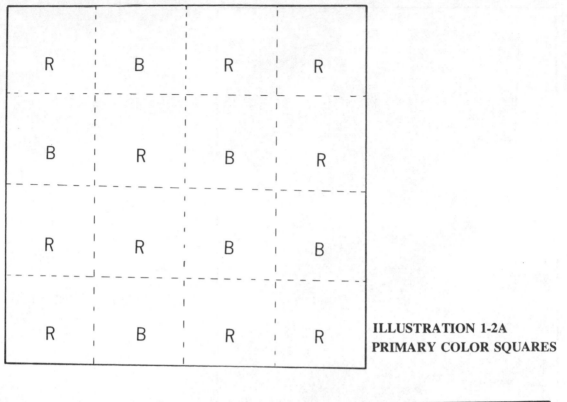

**ILLUSTRATION 1-2A**
**PRIMARY COLOR SQUARES**

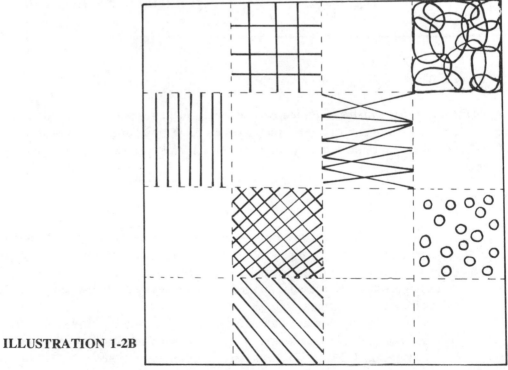

**ILLUSTRATION 1-2B**

- Repeat the procedures and color with the red and yellow crayons on another folded square.
- Color and design the third square with yellow and blue crayons. *Note:* Encourage children to vary the designs in the spaces so that designs will not look exactly like those on the other squares.
- Have the children paste their three designed squares on their construction paper. (See Illustration 1-3.) *Note:* Display the compositions. Help children make comparisons: Which background color makes the reds in the designs seem brightest? The yellows in the designs seem brightest? What happens to the blues on a blue background? How does white affect the compositions?

**ILLUSTRATION 1-3   A PANEL OF PRIMARY SQUARES**

*Can You Imagine . . .*

Make a collection of scraps of cloth, gift wrapping paper, and greeting cards that illustrate the use of blue on blue, red on red, and yellow on yellow.

Cover a wall with 6″ squares (unmounted) of the same color combination in groups of fours to form 12″ × 12″ panels.

Display the following prints and observe color on the same color: Picasso's *La Casserole Emailée* (blue on blue), Matisse's *The Red Studio* (red on red), Van Gogh's *Sunflowers* (yellow on yellow).

## PRIMARY COLORS IN REPETITION (GRADES 5-6)

To create the illusion of color changes by color placement.

*You'll Need . . .*

Red, yellow, and blue construction paper 9″ × 12″ (1 sheet of each color per child) scissors • transparent tape • shirt board or cardboard 8″ × 12″ • paste • paste brushes or dabbers.

*Procedures . . .*

- Divide each sheet of construction paper into 16 equal strips by folding it in half four times along the width.
- Cut the strips apart on the folds.
- Explain to the class that a color can appear to change when placed between two other colors. Illustrate this by taping a red strip between two yellow strips on the chalkboard. (See Illustration 1-4.) Slightly overlap the edges of the center strip. Then tape a red strip between two blue strips (Illustration 1-5). Ask children to observe the two reds. Compare them. Try to determine which appears brighter.
- Tape two yellow strips over a red strip so that only a very thin strip of red is visible. (See Illustration 1-6.) Have children compare this red with the other two. Explain that the amount of color seen also determines how a color appears or looks to the viewer.
- Have the children experiment with arranging their strips on the shirt board. *Note:* Explain that the amount of color shown and the arrangement of the strips should vary. Encourage the children to try various arrangements.
- Paste the strips in the desired arrangement on the cardboard. *Note:* Successful arrangements will have the strips overlapped so that a variety of widths are created. (See Illustration 1-7.)

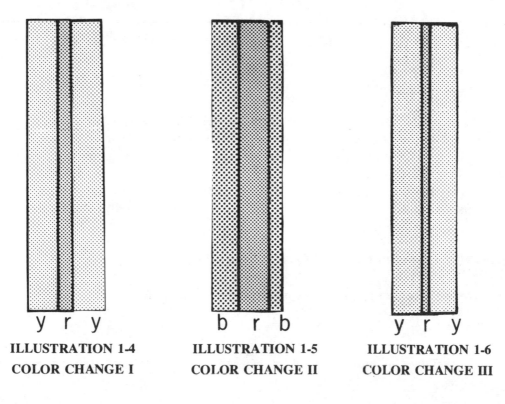

| y  r  y | b  r  b | y  r  y |
|:---:|:---:|:---:|
| **ILLUSTRATION 1-4** | **ILLUSTRATION 1-5** | **ILLUSTRATION 1-6** |
| **COLOR CHANGE I** | **COLOR CHANGE II** | **COLOR CHANGE III** |

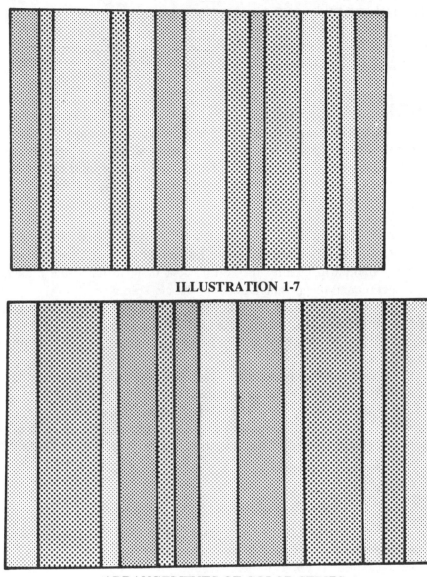

**ILLUSTRATION 1-7**

**ARRANGEMENTS OF COLOR STRIPS**

- Encourage evaluation of the compositions: When does yellow appear brightest? Does yellow ever have a greenish look or cast? When? Does red ever look violet? When? When does blue appear bright? Dull?

*Can You Imagine . . .*

Mount "Primary Colors in Repetition" end to end on a common white background to create a border of primary color effects for an interesting display.

Do the experiment with crayons on shirt board.

Do crayoned representations of striped designs in the children's clothes. Try to determine which set of stripes is brightest and why.

## DISCOVERING ORANGE, GREEN, AND VIOLET (GRADES K-2)

To create other colors with different combinations of red, yellow, and blue.

*You'll Need . . .*

Collection of real and/or artificial items of secondary colors: oranges (3 or 4); eggplant; purple grapes; green plant with many leaves (fern or a vine plant); green, orange, or violet cloth about 3″ × 5″ or gift wrapping paper or a cloth containing all three colors; purple and/or orange flowers • manila paper 9″ × 12″ and 12″ × 18″ • red, yellow, blue crayons.
*Note:* Other orange, green, and violet items may be substituted in the collection.

*Procedures . . .*

- Display the collection of items on a table where each child may see them without difficulty. Ask the children to identify the colors. Ask them to name the orange objects in the collection and other orange items in the classroom.
- Have children experiment with making an orange color on the 9″ × 12″ manila paper by coloring red on yellow until they arrive at an identifiable orange.
- Repeat the procedure for coloring blue on yellow to make green and for coloring blue on red to make violet.
- On the 12″ × 18″ manila paper, with yellow crayon have the children draw all the objects they see on the table. *Note:* Encourage them to make large drawings.
- Have children color their drawings the same color as the objects displayed by blending the primary colors. (See Illustration 1-8.) *Note:* Encourage children to use their manila paper for reference on how they experimented with creating the secondary colors.

*Can You Imagine . . .*

Cover completely the 9″ × 12″ manila paper with orange, green and violet by blending the primary colors. Draw an outdoor scene with black crayon over the colors.

Blend on manila paper the primary colors to make orange, green, or violet. Completely cover the paper with the color. Tear the paper into small pieces. Arrange and paste them in the shape of an animal on construction paper of the same color as one of the primary colors used.

Use these prints to show how artists mix oranges, greens, and violets: Paul Klee's *Dynamism of a Head* and Auguste Renoir's *Girl with Watering Can*.

## STACKING THE SECONDARY (GRADES 3-4)

To build a color on color on color design in order to experience several effects of color placement.

**ILLUSTRATION 1-8   STILL LIFE ARRANGEMENT OF SECONDARY COLORS**

*You'll Need . . .*

Orange, green and violet construction paper 6″ × 9″ (1 color of each per child) • white construction paper 9″ × 12″ • scissors • paste • paste dabbers or brushes.

*Procedures . . .*

- Briefly emphasize the meaning of *secondary* in relation to colors, i.e., a secondary color is a mixture of two primary colors. Show the construction paper for the children to identify the secondary colors.
- Have the children fold the white construction paper into six equal parts.
- Free cut a variety of shapes of different sizes from the 3 sheets of colored construction paper. *Note:* The largest shapes cut should be slightly smaller than ¹/₆ part of the folded white paper.
- In each part or box on the white construction paper (working from left to right), paste a shape of the same color. (See Illustration 1-9A.) *Note:* The color must be the same for each box.

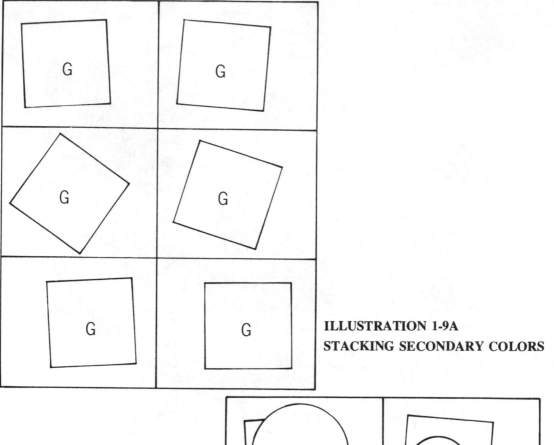

**ILLUSTRATION 1-9A**
**STACKING SECONDARY COLORS**

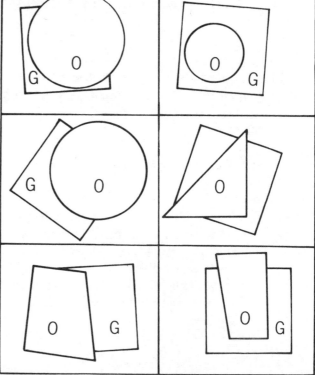

**ILLUSTRATION 1-9B**

- In each box on the previous shape, paste a shape that is a different color. (See Illustration 1-9B.) *Note:* This shape must partly overlap the shape under it so that the previous one is visible.
- In the second through the sixth box, paste a shape that is the third secondary color. (See Illustration 1-9C.) *Note:* This shape must overlap the last attached shape and all shapes previously pasted must be visible. Remind children of these two points as they perform the succeeding steps.
- In the third through the sixth box, paste a shape of a color that is different from the color used last. (See Illustration 1-9D.)
- In the fourth through the sixth box, paste a shape of a color that differs from the color of the previous shape. (See Illustration 1-9E.)
- In the fifth and sixth boxes, paste a shape of a color different from the previous color. (See Illustration 1-9F.) *Note:* At this point, encourage the children to examine their arrangements and make sure that they have used each secondary color at least twice.
- In the sixth box, paste a shape of a color that differs from the previous one. (See Illustration 1-9G.) *Note:* Ask questions to help children do an analysis of their work: Does orange seem brighter when it is between green and violet or between green and green? When does green seem brighter? When does violet seem brighter?

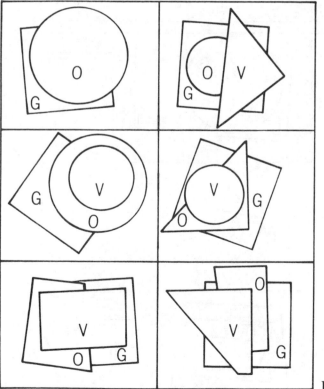

**ILLUSTRATION 1-9C**

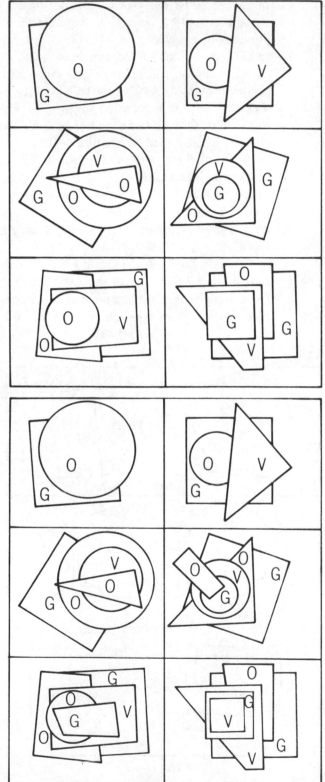

**ILLUSTRATION 1-9D**

**ILLUSTRATION 1-9E**

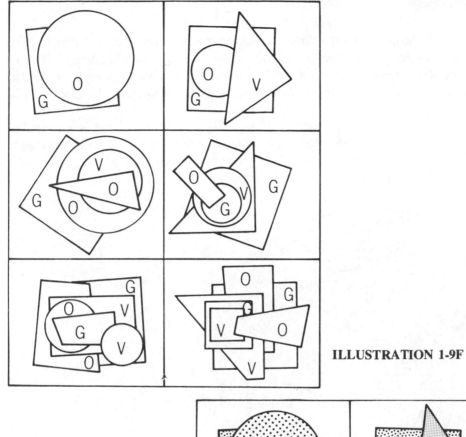

**ILLUSTRATION 1-9F**

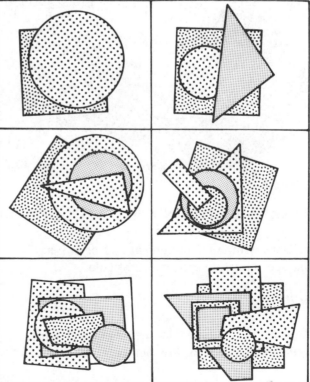

**ILLUSTRATION 1-9G**

*Can You Imagine . . .*

Do a bull's eye design using the three secondary colors. Start with a 9″ circle. Paste smaller circles of the secondary colors on top of the large circle. (See Illustration 1-10.)

Use these prints to show children how artists use secondary colors: George Inness' *The Coming Storm*, Pablo Picasso's *Leaning Harlequin*, and Andre Derain's *Landscape, The Blue Oak*.

Have a "Secondary Day." Ask each child to bring in any object that is a secondary color. On a table, place several of the objects one in front of the other, alternating the colors. Make several still life displays in this manner on separate tables for children to choose one to draw with crayon on manila paper.

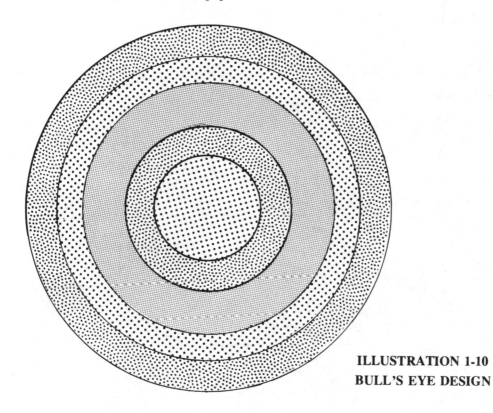

**ILLUSTRATION 1-10**
**BULL'S EYE DESIGN**

## SECONDARY REPETITION AND EFFECTS (GRADES 5-6)

To experiment with color placement and determine the effects of the background on the advancing and retreating appearance of color.

*You'll Need . . .*

One-inch and 2″ cardboard squares (1 of each size per child) • pencils • red, yellow, blue, orange, green and violet construction paper 6″ × 9″ (1 of each color per child) • scissors •

manila paper 6″ × 9″ • paste • paste dabbers or brushes • white cards 3″ × 5″ (6 per child) • white construction paper 6″ × 8″.

*Procedures . . .*

- Using the 1″ and 2″ cardboard squares for patterns, have children trace with a pencil around the squares on the colored construction paper to make 2 each of the following: one-inch squares of orange, green, and violet; and two-inch squares of red, yellow, and blue.
- Cut out the squares. *Note:* Ask the children to look at one of the orange squares and think of the two primary colors that can be mixed to make orange. Encourage them to experiment with blending crayons on the manila paper to make orange. Explain that orange is a secondary color.
- Have the children paste a 1″ orange square in the center of a 2″ red square. (See Illustration 1-11A.)
- Paste this combination of orange and red squares in the center of one of the white cards. (See Illustration 1-11B.)
- Paste the other orange square in the center of a 2″ yellow square. (See Illustration 1-12A.)
- Paste this combination on a white card (Illustration 1-12B).
- Use the above procedures for selecting the colors that make green and for mounting green on yellow and on blue.

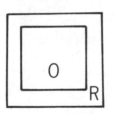

**ILLUSTRATION 1-11A**
**ORANGE ON RED**

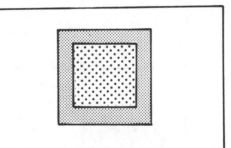

**ILLUSTRATION 1-11B**

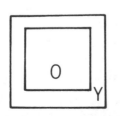

**ILLUSTRATION 1-12A**
**ORANGE ON YELLOW**

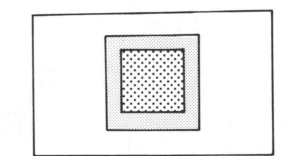

**ILLUSTRATION 1-12B**

- Paste the combination of green and yellow squares on a white card.
- Paste the combination of green and blue squares on a white card.
- Paste one violet square on the blue square and the other violet square on the red. *Note:* Remind the children violet can be made by blending blue and red.
- Paste each combination on a white card. *Note:* Have the children hold the two cards side by side and look through nearly closed eyes at the violet squares. Ask which violet square seems brighter? Which seems farther away? Does one violet square seem larger than the other? (If the response is yes, ask which one.) Which square appears dull? Which square seems more violet? Have the children compare the mounted green squares and the orange squares in the same way.
- Have children put away all the cards except the pair containing a secondary color of their choice.
- Using the 2″ square cardboard pattern, children trace and cut out six 2″ squares from each of the two pieces of construction paper that are of the primary colors on which the selected secondary color is mounted.
- Make a checkerboard by pasting these 2″ squares of primary colors on the white construction paper as suggested in Illustration 1-13A.
- Cut the following from the construction paper of the selected secondary color: 2

**ILLUSTRATION 1-13A**

**RED AND YELLOW CHECKERBOARD WITH ORANGE COUNTERS**

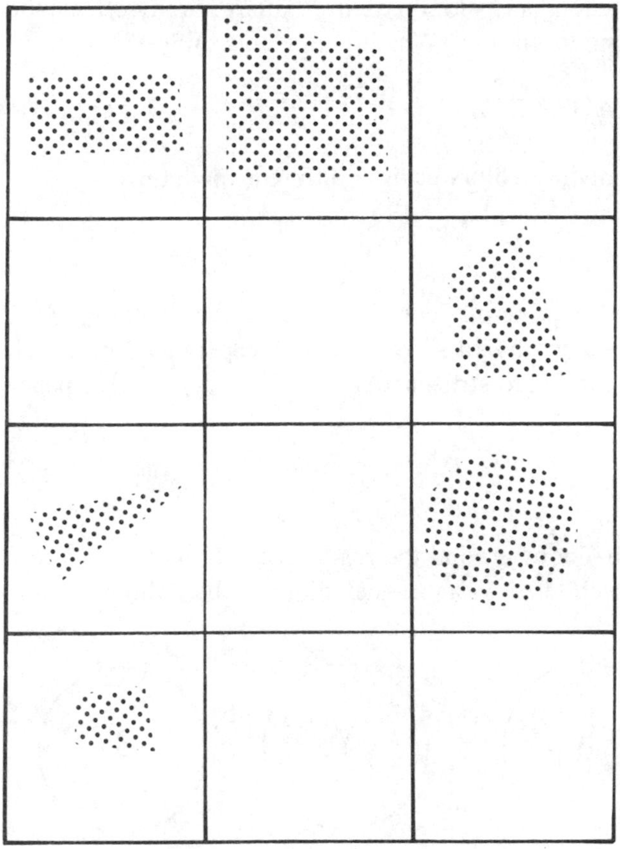

**ILLUSTRATION 1-13B**

large shapes (4-sided, 2-sided, or circular) slightly smaller than a 2″ square on the checkerboard, 2 medium sized shapes, and 2 very small shapes.

• Paste these shapes on six squares on the checkerboard—three on one primary color and three on the other primary color—leaving some empty squares mixed in with those that contain shapes. (See Illustration 1-13B.) *Note:* If the squares are not aligned perfectly, this will not affect the success of this experiment.

• Have a discussion about which arrangements of color and shape give the best examples of secondary color changes.

*Can You Imagine . . .*

On white construction paper, paste 2″ construction paper squares of the primary colors. Paste various sized shapes of only one secondary color on each of the squares. Study the effect of all primary colors upon one secondary color.

Look at these prints to see how artists use primary and secondary colors: Mondrian's *Landscape with Farmhouse*, Odilon Redon's *Vase of Flowers*, Gauguin's *Tahitian Landscape*.

On white construction paper, paste three 2″ construction paper squares of only one primary color. Paste a 1″ square of each secondary color on each 2″ square. Study effects the pairs of colors produce: Which pair seems to vibrate? Which pair seems dullest?

## SIX COLORS IN THE CIRCUS (GRADES K-2)

To experiment with the primary and secondary colors using a different medium.

*You'll Need . . .*

Several colorful circus pictures and a print of Seurat's *Circus* • red, yellow, blue, orange, green, and violet inflated balloons • cardboard 9″ × 12″ • 3 tablespoons • 1 pint each of red, yellow, and blue tempera paint • cardboard strips about 1″ × 2″ (9 per child) • paper towels • newspaper want ad sections.

*Procedures . . .*

- Display the circus pictures and balloons around the room to create a circus atmosphere. Discuss the pictures. Ask children to name the colors of the balloons.

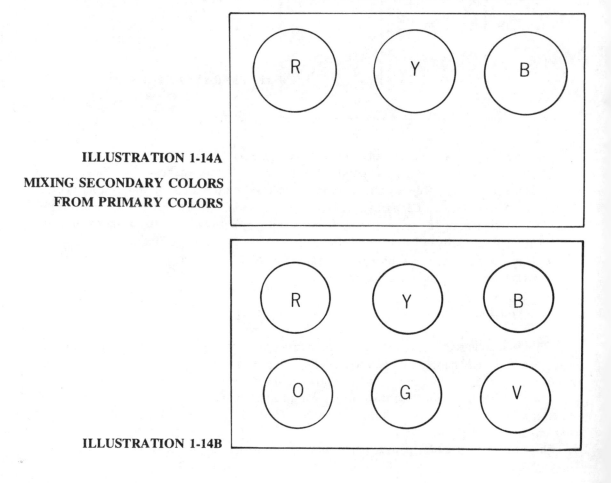

**ILLUSTRATION 1-14A**

**MIXING SECONDARY COLORS
FROM PRIMARY COLORS**

**ILLUSTRATION 1-14B**

- On each child's cardboard, which serves as his palette, put about 2 tablespoons (a tablespoon in different spots) of each of the primary colors of paint. (See Illustration 1-14A.)
- With the cardboard strips, have children mix the secondary colors on their palettes (Illustration 1-14B) as you review with them mixing procedures (described in ''Before You Begin''). *Note:* Remind children to use clean cardboard paint strips when mixing a new color. They put their used strips on a paper towel for painting with those same colors later.
- Have each child paint a full-length self-portrait on the newspaper page. (See Illustration 1-15A.) *Note:* In their paintings, encourage children to try to duplicate the colors they're wearing. Also, remind them, when changing to a different color, to paint with the cardboard strip used before with that color, or to paint with a clean paint strip. Children may work on the desk or on the floor. Use the approach most comfortable for the children and most manageable for you.

**ILLUSTRATION 1-15A**

- Have children paint circus pictures in the remaining space of the newspaper page so that the self-portrait appears to be a part of the circus setting. (See Illustration

1-15B.) *Note:* Encourage them to use all the primary and secondary colors in their paintings.

**ILLUSTRATION 1-15B
SELF-PORTRAIT IN A CIRCUS**

*Can You Imagine . . .*

Use the primary and secondary colors to paint self-portraits into other settings: a birthday party, a parade, the playground.

With the primary and secondary colors, paint a "Balloon Clown" on newspaper. Make the clown colorful. Fill the background with different colored balloons.

Visit the art museum to see Matisse's *Narcissi and Fruit*, Renoir's *In the Meadow* and Paul Klee's *Brother and Sister*. Identify colors and discuss the use of the primary and secondary colors in the paintings.

## A BLOCK OF COLORS (GRADES 3-4)

To use the primary and secondary colors individually and collectively to create a continuous flow of color.

*You'll Need . . .*

Paper towels • small boxes, with flap top lid, varying in sizes from 3″ × 3″ × 3″ to 6″ × 6″ × 6″ (1 per child) • paste • paste dabbers or brushes • 4 pints of white tempera paint • 4 paint brushes • waxed paper (1′ length per child) • 3 tablespoons • 1 pint each of red, yellow, and blue tempera paint • cardboard 9″ × 12″ • 4 tablespoons • cardboard strips 1″ × 2″ • paper towels • pencils.

*Procedures . . .*

- Have children tear paper towels into small sections not to exceed 1″ × 1½″.
- Close and paste down the lid on the box.
- Paste the pieces of paper towel on the box so that every piece overlaps a part of another. (See Illustration 1-16.) *Note:* For a smooth surface for painting, all edges should be pasted down securely.

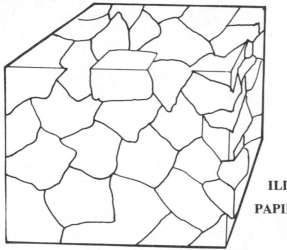

**ILLUSTRATION 1-16**
**PAPIER MÂCHÉ-COVERED BOX**

- Place the white tempera paint and the paint brushes on a table and have groups of four children paint their boxes with the white paint. *Note:* Put waxed paper under each child's box to catch paint drippings and to hold the painted box as it is carried back to the desk.
- Put 2 tablespoons of each primary color of tempera paint on the cardboard palette (a tablespoon in a different spot as shown in Illustration 1-14A, page 32).
- With the cardboard strips the children mix the secondary colors (Illustration 1-14B, page 32) on their palettes. *Note:* Review the procedures for making the secondary colors as described in "Before You Begin." Remind children to use clean cardboard paint strips when mixing a new color. Put used cardboard strips on a paper towel for painting with those same colors later.
- As soon as the white paint dries on the boxes, have children draw pencilled line designs swirling over and around the entire box. (See Illustration 1-17A.)
- Use all six colors on the palette to paint the pencilled design on the box. (See

Illustration 1-17B.) *Note:* Remind children, when changing to a different color, to paint with the cardboard strip used before with that color, or to paint with a clean paint strip if the color is being used for the first time. At some point, a side of the box should be allowed to dry so that the box may rest on that side in order to complete the painting.

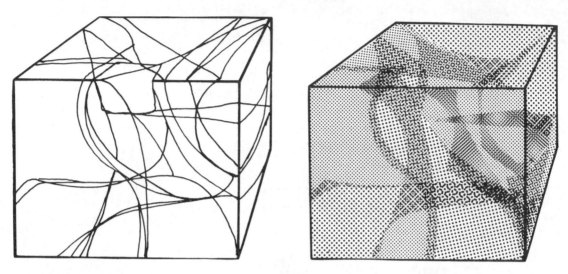

**ILLUSTRATION 1-17A  A BLOCK OF COLORS**          **ILLUSTRATION 1-17B**

*Can You Imagine . . .*

Display the blocks of color in interesting and irregularly stacked arrangements in somber places around the room.

Create a wall of blocks of color by mounting them on a single board or border.

Visit the art museum to see Paul Gauguin's *Tahitian Mountains*, Wassily Kandinsky's *Composition 4*, and Van Gogh's *Walk in the Evening*. Discuss use of the primary and secondary colors in these compositions. Observe other prints with dominant primary and secondary colors.

## COLOR ME PRIMARY AND SECONDARY (GRADES 5-6)

To emphasize the relationship of the primary colors to the secondary colors by using them as the composition.

*You'll Need . . .*

Newspaper • 1 pint each of red, yellow, and blue tempera paint • 3 tablespoons • white crayons or rubber cement (if rubber cement is used, have available paste brushes or small sticks or pieces of tongue depressors and pencil erasers) • white construction paper 4″ × 6″ (6 per child) • cardboard 9″ × 12″ • cardboard strips about 1″ × 2″ (9 per child) • paper towels • paste • paste dabbers or brushes • white construction paper 18″ × 24″.

*Procedures . . .*

*Note:* Set up a newspaper covered table or other area containing the mixed tempera paint and tablespoons.

- Write the names of the primary and secondary colors on the chalkboard.
- Cover the desks with newspaper.
- Have children use white crayon (or rubber cement) to write a color name on each small piece of white construction paper. (See Illustration 1-18A.) *Note:* The white crayon or rubber cement must be applied heavily to make the letters wide or thick. Letters should not touch. If rubber cement is used, allow it to dry before paint is applied.

**ILLUSTRATION 1-18A  ADDING COLOR TO COLOR WORDS**

- Put 2 tablespoons of each primary color on the cardboard palette (a tablespoon in a different spot as shown in Illustration 1-14A, page 32).
- With the cardboard strips, have children mix the secondary colors on their palettes (Illustration 1-14B, p. 32). *Note:* Review mixing procedures described in ''Before You Begin.'' Remind children to use clean cardboard paint strips when mixing a new color. Put used strips on a paper towel for painting with those colors later.

- With the cardboard strips, paint each small piece of white construction paper the color that is written on it. *Note:* The paint will not take on the crayon or rubber cement. Therefore, all the space surrounding the word will be in color as shown in Illustration 1-18B.

**ILLUSTRATION 1-18B**

- After the paint dries, arrange and paste the six compositions on the 18″ × 24″ white construction paper. (See Illustration 1-19.) *Note:* Corners of the compositions may touch. Compositions may be arranged in different positions. Encourage originality in arrangements. If rubber cement was used, have children rub off the cement with a pencil eraser or a finger.

*Can You Imagine . . .*

Substitute on the rectangles other words that can be associated with colors, such as *Spring* for green, and *fire* for red.

Make book covers with this technique.

Visit the art museum to see Paul Cezanne's *Vase of Flowers*, Henri Matisse's *Odalisque*, and Marin's *The Singer Building*. Observe these and other prints to discover how artists use primary and secondary colors in composition.

**ILLUSTRATION 1-19   COMPOSITION OF COLORS AND THEIR NAMES**

# CHAPTER 2

# WARM AND COOL COLORS

Each of the primary and secondary colors can be classified as warm or cool. Warm colors appear to generate heat and suggest excitement and noise. Primary colors red and yellow along with orange, a secondary color, are basically warm. The sun, a fire, a cheering crowd, and a circus band often are associated with warm colors. Can you imagine feeling great warmth from a blue sun or a green fire?

Cool colors seem to have quieter qualities and usually represent the tranquil side of things. The primary color blue, and the secondary colors green and violet are generally considered cool. Peace, serenity, twilight, and mystery usually are illustrated with cool colors. An orange twilight, a yellow snow fall, or a bright red haunted house would completely destroy any ideas of serenity, quietness, or mystery.

This chapter contains color projects that give children opportunities to work with color classifications and observe effects of using these categories jointly and independently.

**BEFORE YOU BEGIN**

Display three or four of the color wheels the children made. (See Chapter 1, "Before You Begin.") Point to *red* on a color wheel. Ask the children to name something that reminds them of this color. (Expect a variety of responses: stop signs, fire trucks, the sun, etc.) Repeat this procedure for orange and yellow. Explain that these three colors—red, orange, and yellow—are called warm colors.

Ask what is the opposite of warm.

Point to *green* on a color wheel. Have the children name objects that they associate with this color. Repeat this procedure for blue and violet. Explain that these colors—green, blue, and violet—are called cool colors. On the color wheel, the cool colors are across or opposite the warm colors. (See Figure 2-1.)

To assist children in "feeling" warm and cool colors so that they may begin to use these color groupings more, play this association game.

Give each child red, yellow, orange, blue, green, and violet crayons and a sheet of manila paper 9″ × 12″.

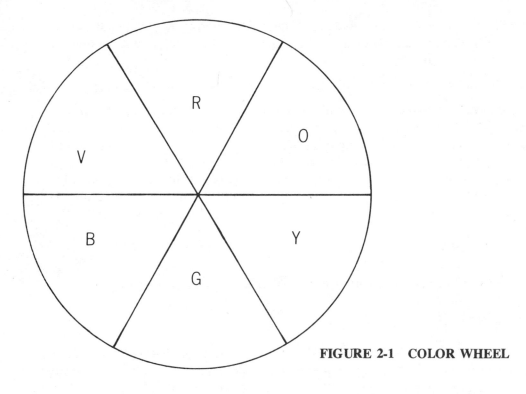

**FIGURE 2-1   COLOR WHEEL**

| | |
|---|---|
| 1 | 9 |
| 2 | 10 |
| 3 | 11 |
| 4 | 12 |
| 5 | 13 |
| 6 | 14 |
| 7 | 15 |
| 8 | 16 |

**FIGURE 2-2**

**PAGE FOR**

**COLOR ASSOCIATION GAME**

Holding the paper vertically, fold in half three times horizontally. Open the paper and fold it in half once vertically. (See Figure 2-2.) From top to bottom number the spaces 1 to 16.

Ask the children to separate their six crayons into warm and cool groups.

Say the word *smile* and ask the children if it makes them think of a warm or cool color. Say: "If smile reminds you of a warm color, select one of the warm colors of crayon and make a patch of color in space 1. If you think of a cool color, select a color from the cool group of crayons and make the color patch." Continue with these words for the other spaces: (2) friend, (3) work, (4) love, (5) shadow, (6) wet, (7) Mother, (8) dream, (9) sadness, (10) you (the child), (11) autumn, (12) wind, (13) surprise, (14) toothache, (15) music, and (16) kindness.

## COLOR IT WARM (GRADES K-2)

To create a repetitious arrangement of a familiar shape with emphasis on color.

*You'll Need . . .*

Poems about rain ("The Umbrella Brigade" by Laura E. Richards, "Rain" by Robert Lewis Stevenson, etc.) • a brightly colored umbrella • orange, red, and yellow construction paper 9″ × 12″ (1 color of each per child) • orange, red, and yellow crayons (1 color of each per child) • scissors • gray bogus paper 20″ × 15″ • paste • paste dabbers or brushes • a black or gray umbrella.

*Procedures . . .*

- Talk about a rainy day. Read the poems about rain to the class. Discuss the color of the sky on a rainy day. *Note:* Try to have this lesson on a rainy day so that children can see what is meant by "a gray day."
- Show the children the brightly colored umbrella. Encourage them to feel and describe its texture, identify its color or colors, and discuss its shape when closed and open.
- Draw a large circle, square, and triangle on the chalkboard.
- Hold the brightly colored umbrella as shown in Illustration 2-1 for the children to see. Ask if it reminds them of any one of the shapes drawn on the chalkboard.
- Change a side of the triangle on the chalkboard to resemble the scalloped edge of the view of the umbrella.
- On a sheet of the construction paper with crayon, have children draw the closed umbrella and cut it out. *Note:* Encourage them to make a big shape, at least 4″ in length. Demonstrate the approximate size by cutting the umbrella shape. Children may free cut the shape without drawing it.
- Turn the umbrella in different positions (Illustrations 2-2, 2-3, 2-4, 2-5, 2-6, and 2-7) and have the children draw and cut out each view. *Note:* If children understood and carried out the previous procedure, it will not be necessary to draw these views

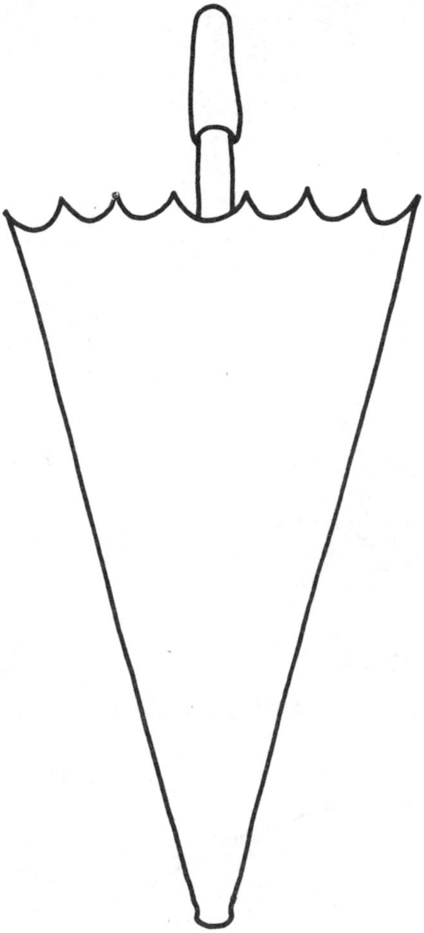

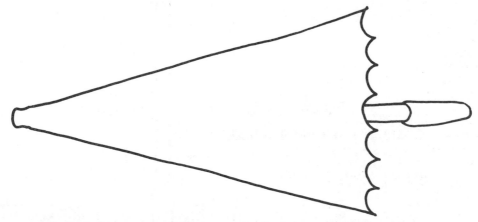

**ILLUSTRATION 2-1
UPRIGHT VIEW
OF CLOSED UMBRELLA**

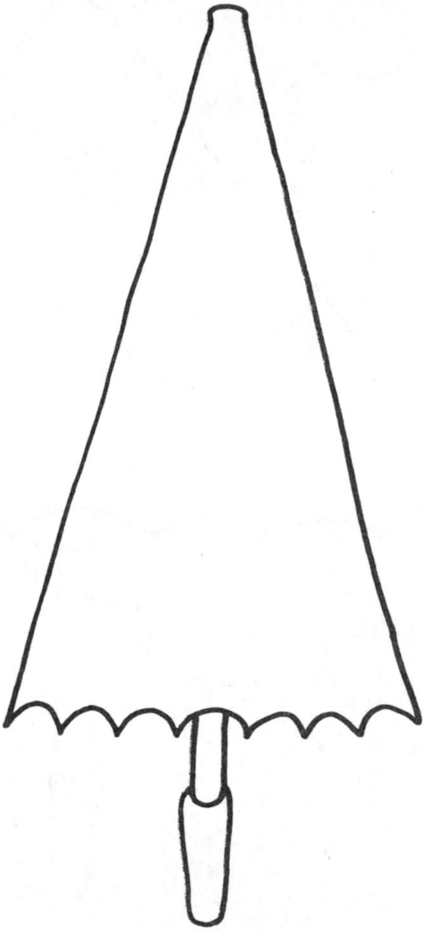

**ILLUSTRATION 2-2
INVERTED VIEW
OF CLOSED UMBRELLA**

**ILLUSTRATION 2-3   HORIZONTAL VIEW OF CLOSED UMBRELLA**

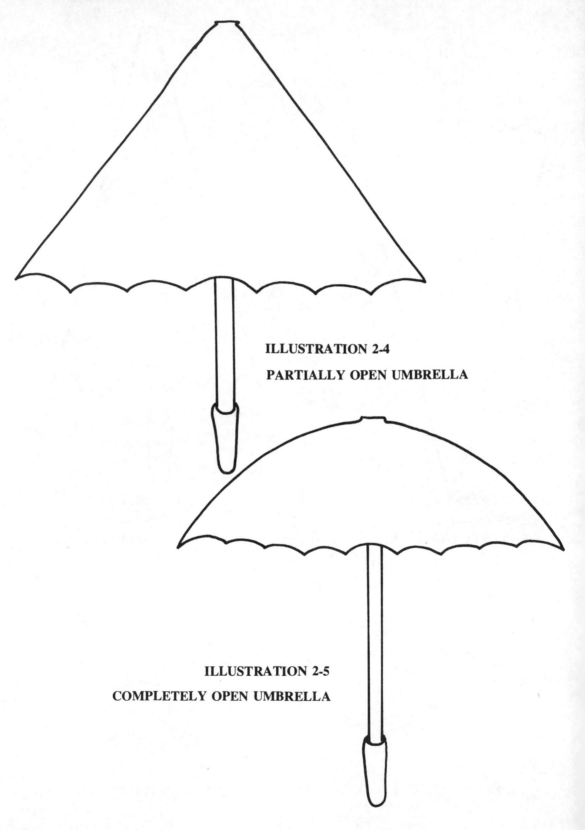

**ILLUSTRATION 2-4**

**PARTIALLY OPEN UMBRELLA**

**ILLUSTRATION 2-5**

**COMPLETELY OPEN UMBRELLA**

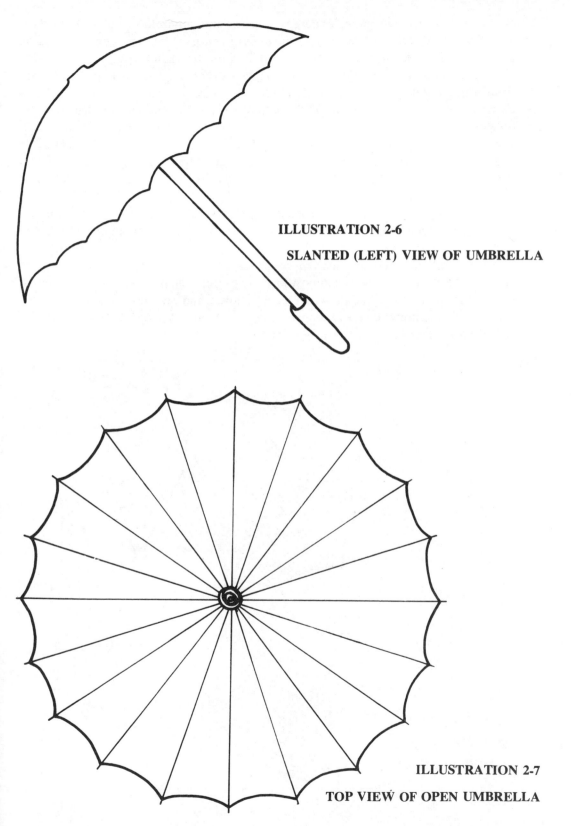

**ILLUSTRATION 2-6**

**SLANTED (LEFT) VIEW OF UMBRELLA**

**ILLUSTRATION 2-7**

**TOP VIEW OF OPEN UMBRELLA**

on the chalkboard. Encourage children to make some umbrellas smaller than others and to use all three colors of paper. Have them compare the last view (Illustration 2-7) with the circle, square, and triangle drawn on the chalkboard.

- Have children cut additional umbrella shapes in order to have a larger collection from which to choose for an arrangement.
- Experiment with arrangements of the umbrellas on the gray bogus paper. *Note:* Shapes may or may not touch or overlap. Encourage arrangements that have red, yellow, and orange umbrellas mingled together.
- Paste the desired arrangement of shapes on the bogus paper. (See Illustration 2-8A.)
- With the left-over orange, yellow, and red scraps, free cut stripes, polka dots, and other designs.
- Paste the designs on the umbrella shapes. (See Illustration 2-8B.) *Note:* All umbrellas need not have designs. Suggest using a design of color other than the color of the umbrella.
- Make umbrella handles with the crayons. (See Illustration 2-8C.)
- Have the children study their compositions of umbrella shapes. Ask why it is a good idea to have umbrellas that are warm reds, yellows, and oranges. *Note:* Display the brightly colored umbrella along with a gray or black one. Ask the children which one would they rather carry on a gray day and why.

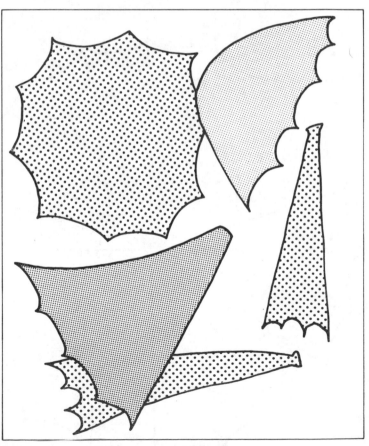

**ILLUSTRATION 2-8A
ARRANGEMENTS OF FREE-
CUT UMBRELLA SHAPES**

**ILLUSTRATION 2-8B**

*Can You Imagine . . .*

Create an umbrella brigade. Paste silhouettes or cutout drawings of people under bright umbrellas.

With crayon, draw a crowd or a line of people on gray bogus paper. From orange, red, and yellow cloth scraps, free cut sweaters, hats, suits, dresses, etc., and paste on the people.

Select only one view of the umbrella. Free cut this shape as many times as possible from the three colors of construction paper. Overlap these shapes in an arrangement on bogus paper and paste in position. Add designs and handles.

## LINES OF COLOR VIBRATIONS (GRADES 3-4)

To create a glowing, sunny composition by using warm colors.

*You'll Need . . .*

Three or 4 of the children's color wheels (see Chapter 1, "Before You Begin") • cloth and felt scraps 2″ × 2″ of reds, yellows, and oranges (5 or 6 scraps that include a mixture of

**ILLUSTRATION 2-8C**

the colors per child) • scissors • paste • paste dabbers or brushes • construction paper 12″ × 18″ of pastel reds, yellows, and oranges (1 piece of paper per child) • crayons or reds, yellows, and oranges (1 of each three colors per child).

*Procedures . . .*

- Display the color wheels. Ask which three of the six colors suggest sunlight (*red, yellow,* and *orange*). Remind the children that these three colors are called *warm colors.*
- Have children change the shapes of their felt and cloth scraps by cutting off or curving some of the edges. (See Illustration 2-9A.)

   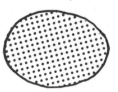 

**ILLUSTRATION 2-9A   ALTERED CLOTH SCRAPS**

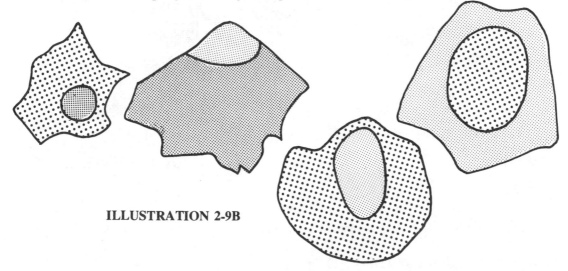

**ILLUSTRATION 2-9A    ALTERED CLOTH SCRAPS (CONTINUED)**

- Paste small shapes on the larger shapes (Illustration 2-9B).

**ILLUSTRATION 2-9B**

- Paste these combined shapes on the construction paper so that no two are on the same level as suggested in Illustration 2-9B. *Note:* All edges should be pasted down securely.
- Add heavily colored stems and leaves to the shapes with the crayons. (See Illustration 2-9C.)
- Draw several crayon lines around the blooms and leaves (Illustration 2-9D). *Note:* Children may alternate colors of lines around a bloom.
- Fill in all background areas with vertical or horizontal lines. (See Illustration 2-9E.) *Note:* This composition is enhanced by strong, dark crayon lines.

*Can You Imagine . . .*

Use this composition or a part of it as decoration for a card or book cover.

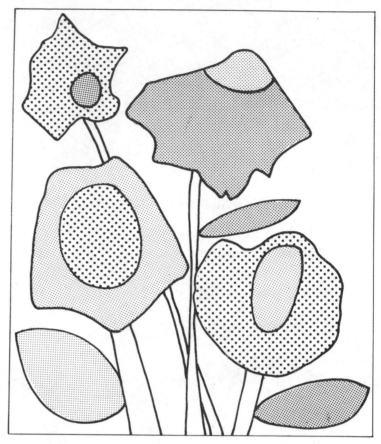

**ILLUSTRATION 2-9C**

Paint the surface of the composition with shellac and mount on white pebble board. Use animals or fish shapes instead of flowers to create "Lines of Color Vibrations."

## WARM ON WARM (GRADES 5-6)

To compare effects of warm colors on warm colors on warm colors.

*You'll Need . . .*

Three or 4 color wheels made by the children (see Chapter 1, "Before You Begin") • 3″ × 5″ cards (6 per child) • red, yellow, and orange construction paper 9″ × 12″ (1 of each color per child plus an extra sheet of one of the three colors of his choice) • pencils • scissors • paste • paste dabbers or brushes • white construction paper 12″ × 12″.

*Procedures . . .*

- Display the color wheels. Help children identify and name the warm colors. Ask them to name various objects that they feel are more effective because warm colors

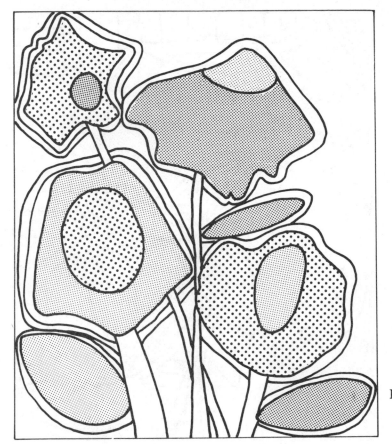

**ILLUSTRATION 2-9D**

are used on the objects. (For example: varied colored park benches instead of green, light yellow schoolroom walls instead of dark blue, red or yellow fire truck instead of black, etc.)

- Have children place a 3″ × 5″ card in one corner of the construction paper of which there are *two* sheets of that color. (See Illustration 2-10.)
- With a pencil trace around the card.
- Cut out the traced shape.
- Cut out five more of these traced shapes from the same color or cut some of the five from the two other colors of construction paper.
- Paste one of these rectangular shapes on each of the six white cards.
- Turn the cards over and on the backs number them consecutively beginning with 2. *Note:* Explain that each numeral indicates the layers of color to be pasted on the front side of the card. Ask how many layers of color do the cards have already. (The answer is *one* because one color has been pasted on each card.)
- Turn up the front side of *card 2* as shown in Illustration 2-11A.
- Cut a smaller rectangle from a piece of construction paper that is different in color from the front side of the card. *Note:* Color of *card 2* will vary among children.
- Paste this smaller rectangle on *card 2.* (See Illustration 2-11B.) *Note:* Ask the

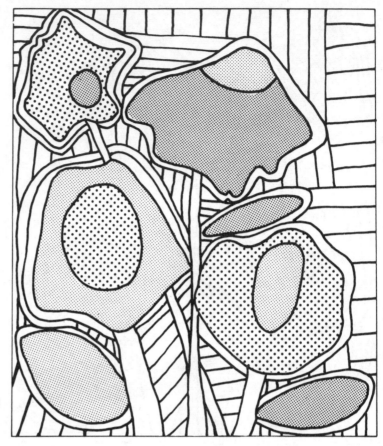

**ILLUSTRATION 2-9E**

children to count the layers of colors on this card. *Card 2* is completed since it now contains two layers of colors.

- Cut the appropriate number of rectangles and paste on *cards 3, 4, 5, 6,* and *7.* (See Illustrations 2-12 to 2-16.) *Note:* Remind children that rectangles added on the different cards can vary in size—but each rectangle must be smaller than the last one pasted on the card so that the rectangles underneath can be seen. Encourage different color arrangements on a card though no two rectangles of the same color should be pasted on top of one another. Remind children to count the layers of colors on each card to be sure they have the number indicated on the back.
- Arrange and paste these six cards on the white construction paper so that they touch each other but do not touch edges of the white paper as suggested in Illustration 2-17.

*Can You Imagine . . .*

Use the design on greeting cards.
Decorate each side of a cube with a different number of stacked shapes of warm colors.
Stack warm colors of felt on burlap to create wall hangings.

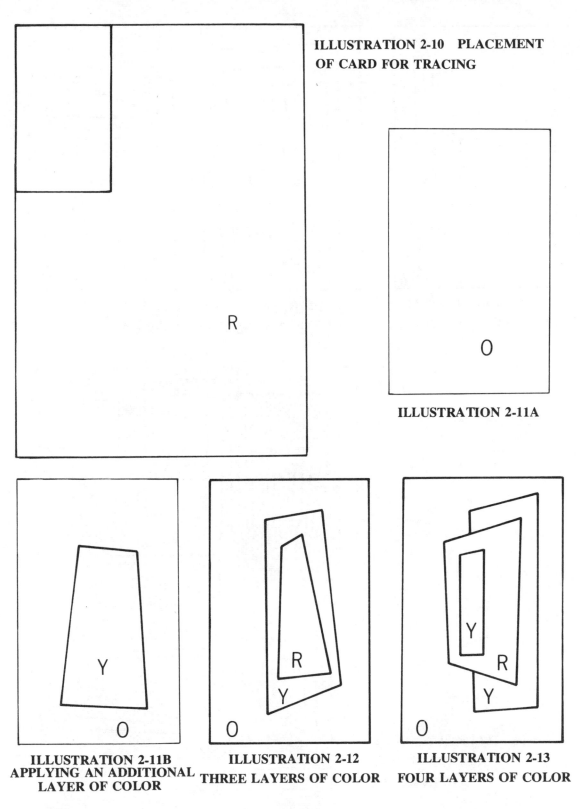

**ILLUSTRATION 2-10   PLACEMENT OF CARD FOR TRACING**

R

O

**ILLUSTRATION 2-11A**

Y

O

**ILLUSTRATION 2-11B APPLYING AN ADDITIONAL LAYER OF COLOR**

R

Y

O

**ILLUSTRATION 2-12 THREE LAYERS OF COLOR**

Y

R

Y

O

**ILLUSTRATION 2-13 FOUR LAYERS OF COLOR**

**ILLUSTRATION 2-14**
**FIVE LAYERS OF COLOR**

**ILLUSTRATION 2-15**
**SIX LAYERS OF COLOR**

**ILLUSTRATION 2-16**
**SEVEN LAYERS OF COLOR**

**ILLUSTRATION 2-17**
**ARRANGEMENT OF**
**COLOR LAYERS**

## A SHOWER OF FLOWERS (GRADES K-2)

To use blue, green, and violet singularly and in various combinations to create compositions.

### You'll Need . . .

Three or 4 color wheels (see Chapter 1, ''Before You Begin'') • scissors • dark violet, dark blue, and dark green construction paper 9″ × 12″ (1 color of each per child) • paste • paste dabbers or brushes • pale violet, sky blue, and light green construction paper 12″ × 18″ (1 color of each child's choice) • green, blue, and violet crayons (1 of each color per child).

### Procedures . . .

- Display the color wheels. Help children identify and name the warm colors (*red, orange, yellow*) and the cool colors (*green, blue,* and *violet*).
- Cut from 9″ × 12″ violet construction paper 3 round shapes of different sizes —approximately 3″, 2″, and 1″ in diameter—to show the class.
- Show the shapes one at a time and have children cut similar shapes from their 9″ × 12″ violet paper. *Note:* Shapes should be of different sizes, but they need not be perfectly round and they do not have to match your models in sizes.
- Have children continue to cut round shapes (Illustration 2-18) of various sizes from all three colors of 9″ × 12″ construction paper. *Note:* Encourage them to cut out as many sizes as possible and to keep all shapes no matter how small they may be.

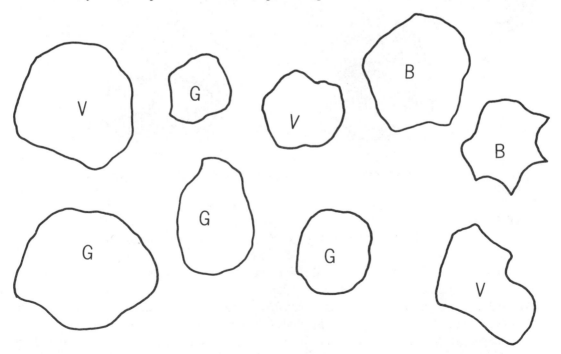

**ILLUSTRATION 2-18   DIFFERENT SIZES OF SHAPES**

- Select one shape from the group and paste a smaller shape of a different color on it. (See Illustration 2-19.)
- Select a large shape and paste two smaller shapes of different sizes and colors on it (Illustration 2-20).

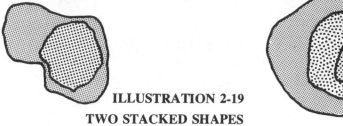

**ILLUSTRATION 2-19**
**TWO STACKED SHAPES**

**ILLUSTRATION 2-20**
**THREE STACKED SHAPES**

- With the remaining shapes, have children paste smaller shapes on larger shapes. *Note:* Encourage them to make as many different color groupings as possible with the three cool colors, such as: green on violet on green, and green on blue. Demonstrate if children seem to need more visual assistance as suggested in Illustration 2-21.

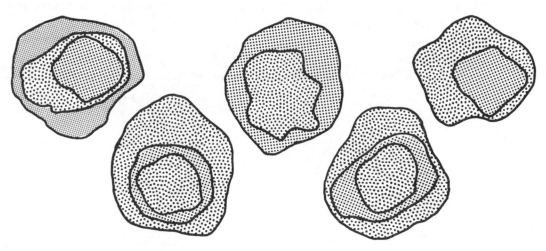

**ILLUSTRATION 2-21   VARIATIONS OF STACKED SHAPES**

- Ask the children to close their eyes and imagine that they see flowers tumbling down. Ask if all stems would point in the same or different directions as the flowers fell.
- Have children paste their stacked shapes in tumbling positions on their selected cool color of the 12″ × 18″ construction paper.
- Add crayon stems and leaves to each flower. (See Illustration 2-22.) *Note:* Encourage use of all three colors of crayons for the stems and leaves. Remind children that stems should point in all directions so that flowers seem to be drifting or floating downward.

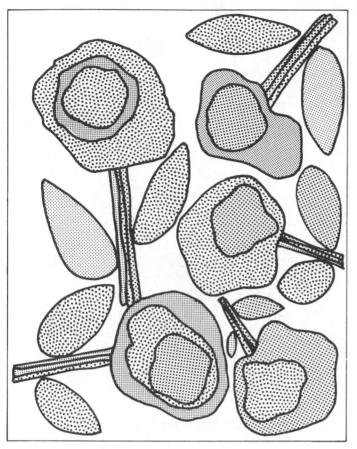

**ILLUSTRATION 2-22**

*Can You Imagine . . .*

Paste stacked circle shapes on a strip of paper and make a headband of flowers.

Cut a large basket shape from a cool color of construction paper. Use some of each child's shapes to fill the "basket" with "flowers" for a bulletin board. Attach a large tag with names of children who have birthdays that month. Include the message: HAPPY BIRTHDAY!

Spell out a greeting (or title, child's name, month, etc.) using these shapes. (See Illustration 2-23.)

## TALL, THIN, AND COOL (GRADES 3-4)

To create a slender arrangement of cool colors within a given area.

*You'll Need . . .*

Manila drawing paper 6″ × 18″ (2 per child) • scissors • 2 or 3 bottles or vases (preferably blue, green, or violet) • blue, green, and violet construction paper 6″ × 18″ (1 of

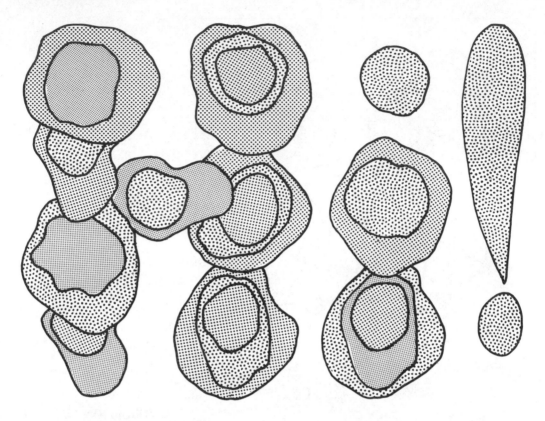

**ILLUSTRATION 2-23   WORDS FROM FLOWERS**

each color per child) • blue, green, and violet crayons (1 of each color per child) • 3″ × 5″ cards • gray bogus paper 20″ × 7½″ • paste • paste dabbers or brushes • blue, green, or violet yarn 36″ lengths (2 lengths per child).

*Procedures . . .*

- Ask the children to identify something in the classroom that is a cool color (*blue, green, violet*). *Note:* Be sure all materials for this lesson are placed on a table or desk ahead of time.
- Fold each piece of manila paper in half lengthwise.
- Display the bottles or vases and call attention to the shape of the mouth, neck, body, and bottom of each.
- Applying the method used to cut out a valentine, have children free cut a different bottle shape from each folded piece of manila paper. (See Illustration 2-24.)
- Place the manila paper shapes on the colored construction paper and trace around them with blue, violet, or green crayon. *Note:* Three or more bottle shapes should be traced on the construction paper, using both patterns or only one.
- Cut out the colored bottle shapes.

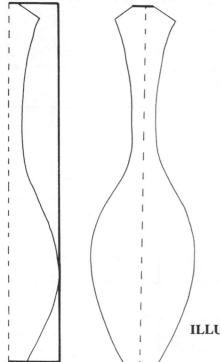

**ILLUSTRATION 2-24   FREE CUT BOTTLE SHAPES**

- Place the 3″ × 5″ card in a corner of the bogus paper and trace around the card with blue, green, or violet crayon. (See Illustration 2-25A.)
- Using this same color of crayon, fill the bogus paper with rectangular shapes by tracing the card in overlapping positions. (See Illustration 2-25B.)
- Trace over all lines to make them darker.
- Lightly color each new shape created, using blue, green, and violet crayons. (See Illustration 2-25C.) *Note:* Encourage children to arrange colors so that all three are used in different areas on the bogus paper.
- Arrange and paste the construction paper bottle shapes on the bogus in overlapping positions so that a portion of each bottle remains visible as suggested in Illustration 2-25D. *Note:* Bottle shapes should not touch or extend over the edges of the bogus paper.
- Paint a thin strip of paste around the visible portion of each bottle shape.
- Press the yarn on the paste outline. *Note:* Cut off any excess yarn after a shape has been outlined with the yarn.

*Can You Imagine . . .*

Surround with yarn not only the bottles but also each rectangle in the composition background.

Instead of bottle shapes, use a shape of a seasonal subject often associated with a cool color: leaf, pine tree (green and blue), buildings and shadows (violet), etc.

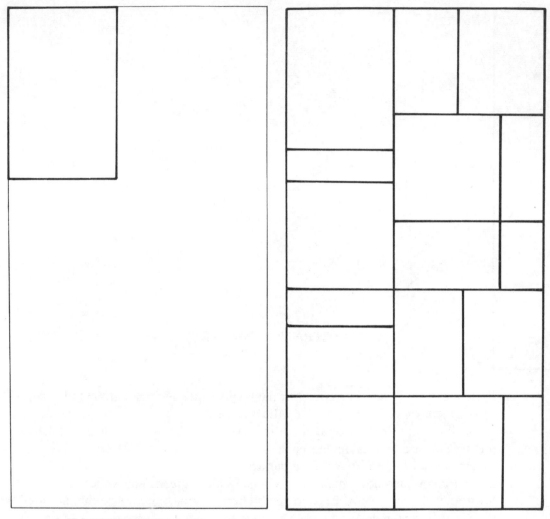

**ILLUSTRATION 2-25A**
**RECTANGULAR AND BOTTLE SHAPES**
**IN COOL COLOR COMBINATION**

**ILLUSTRATION 2-25B**

Begin with procedures for drawing rectangular shapes on bogus paper. Color the newly created shapes as suggested. Place the yarn on the bogus paper so that it forms the shape of a bottle. Paste the yarn in place. Make two other bottles with the yarn.

## COOL ON COOL (GRADES 5-6)

To experiment with grouping cool colors side by side and stacking them.

*You'll Need . . .*

Various shades of green, blue, and violet construction paper 9″ × 12″ (1 of each color per child) • pencils • manila paper 9″ × 12″ • scissors • paste • paste dabbers or brushes.

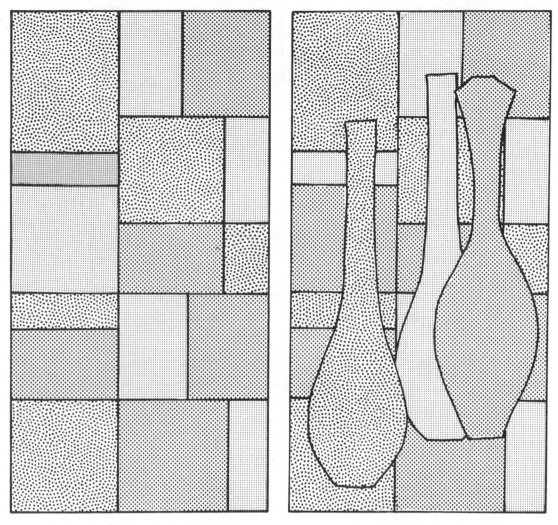

**ILLUSTRATION 2-25C**          **ILLUSTRATION 2-25D**

*Procedures . . .*

- Discuss the meaning of cool colors and ask the children to identify them. (See "Before You Begin.") Explain that a rhythmical arrangement can make these colors appear to change, and that size and placement have a great influence on the way a color appears to the viewer.
- Have children each select three colors of construction paper.
- Number each sheet in one corner. For example, see Illustration 2-26. From this point on, colors of these sheets will be referred to by number instead of the color name, for example, *color 1. Note:* A child may number any color as 1, 2, or 3.
- Fold the manila paper and each sheet of construction paper widthwise in half three times and fold in half once lengthwise. (See Illustration 2-27.)

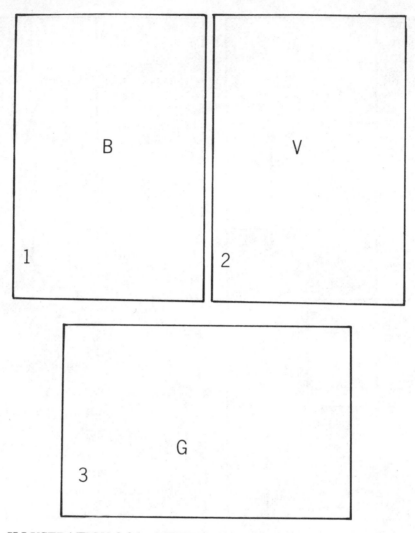

**ILLUSTRATION 2-26  ASSIGNING EACH COLOR A NUMBER**

- Cut *colors 2* and *3* on the folds into the small rectangles.
- Place the manila paper on the desk so that the rows of eight spaces are in horizontal position. *Note:* If the class did the project, "Primary Colors in Repetition," Chapter 1, review how colors were placed beside colors to form a pattern. Also, if they did the project "Warm on Warm" in the first section of this chapter, review how arrangements were made by putting color on color. Explain that the project in this lesson combines both techniques of color arrangements.
- On the manila paper plan an arrangement of colors for the top row of spaces by entering a color number in each space. For example: 12323121 (Illustration 2-28A), 31323123, or 13223121. *Note:* Encourage children to experiment with arrangement of a color plan. They may erase the numbers and replan an arrangement.

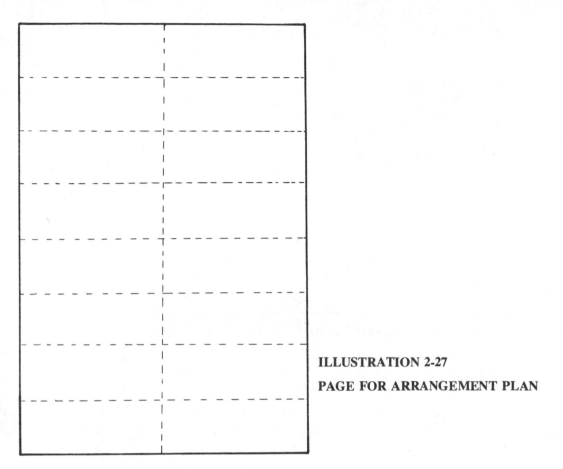

**ILLUSTRATION 2-27**

**PAGE FOR ARRANGEMENT PLAN**

- Record the reverse of the chosen color arrangement in the bottom row of spaces. (See Illustration 2-28B.)
- Place *color 1* horizontally on the desk.
- Follow the color arrangement planned on the manila paper by pasting small colored construction paper rectangles in the spaces of *color 1*. *Note:* Spaces that are planned for *color 1* already contain the correct color since the construction paper is *color 1*. Rectangles of colors 2 and 3 are being pasted on *color 1*. See Illustration 2-29A for an example of an arrangement where blue is *color 1* (and is the color of the whole sheet of paper), violet is *2* and green is *3*. Rectangles should touch the horizontal center fold.
- Cut some of the remaining rectangles of *colors 2* and *3* into fourths and others into eighths.
- Paste these colored shapes in a vertical arrangement on several of *color 1* rectangles and on several of the rectangles pasted on *color 1* themselves to create a color on color composition. (See Illustration 2-29B.) *Note:* Remind children that areas of previously pasted rectangles can become part of the arrangement as shown, for

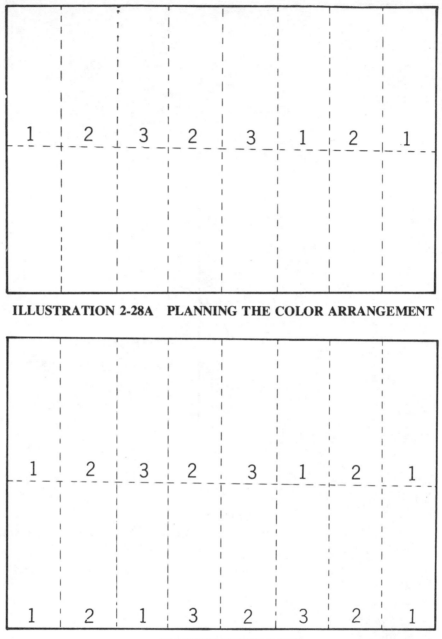

**ILLUSTRATION 2-28A   PLANNING THE COLOR ARRANGEMENT**

**ILLUSTRATION 2-28B**

example, in the second space of the first row and the first space of the second row of Illustration 2-29B.

*Can You Imagine . . .*

Place the ''Cool on Cool'' arrangements on white mat boards and display on walls and bulletin boards. Over a period of time, study the effects of cool colors on each other.

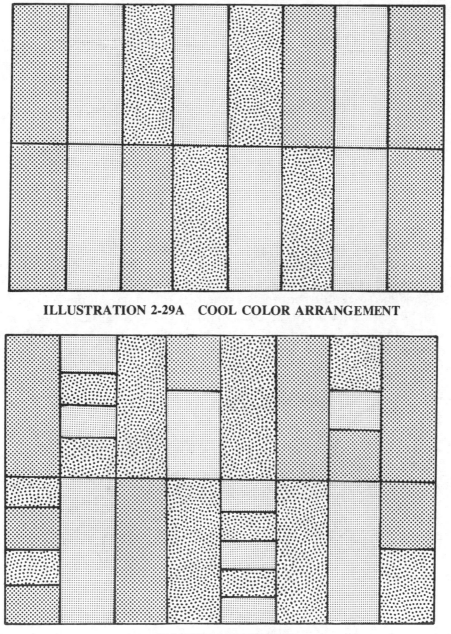

**ILLUSTRATION 2-29A   COOL COLOR ARRANGEMENT**

**ILLUSTRATION 2-29B**

Use the design as a background for bold bright lettering.
Work out a seasonal color arrangement for wall and display borders.

## A COLOR PIE (GRADES K-2)

To group collections of warm and cool colors in a controlled arrangement.

*You'll Need . . .*

One color wheel (see Chapter 1, "Before You Begin") • 10″ bogus paper circles with pencilled divisions into 6 equal triangles (as shown in Figure 1-1 page 13) • paste • paste dabbers or brushes • 1″ shapes cut from red, yellow, blue, orange, green, and violet construction paper (1 of each color per child) • scissors • magazines containing color (1 per child) • white construction paper 18″ × 18″.

*Procedures . . .*

- Display the color wheel. Help the children identify and name the warm colors. Display a bogus circle to the right of the color wheel. Point out *red* on the wheel.
- Paste a small red shape in the triangular space on the bogus circle (Illustration 2-30A) in the space that corresponds with the red triangle on the color wheel.
- Have children paste a small red shape on their bogus circle in like manner.
- Continue to paste the other small colored shapes, one at a time, in the triangular spaces on the large bogus circle and have the children do the same. (See Illustration 2-30B.)

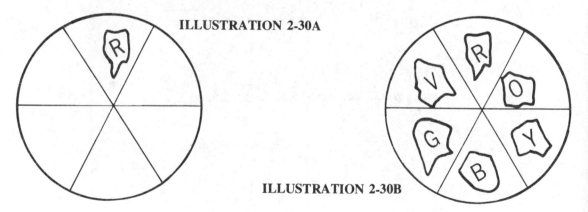

**ILLUSTRATION 2-30A**

**ILLUSTRATION 2-30B**

- Have children cut out small red swatches of color from the magazine. *Note:* Have them compare their cutout colors to observe that all the reds are not alike.
- Paste these red pieces on the bogus circle in the space with the small red circle (Illustration 2-30C). *Note:* Encourage children to fill the space with samples of reds.
- Continue to cut color from the magazine for each color designated by the small colored circle and paste appropriately on the bogus shape. (See Illustration 2-30D.) *Note:* Finding, cutting out, and pasting a color can constitute one session so that the project may be extended over several sessions for kindergarten and first grade children.

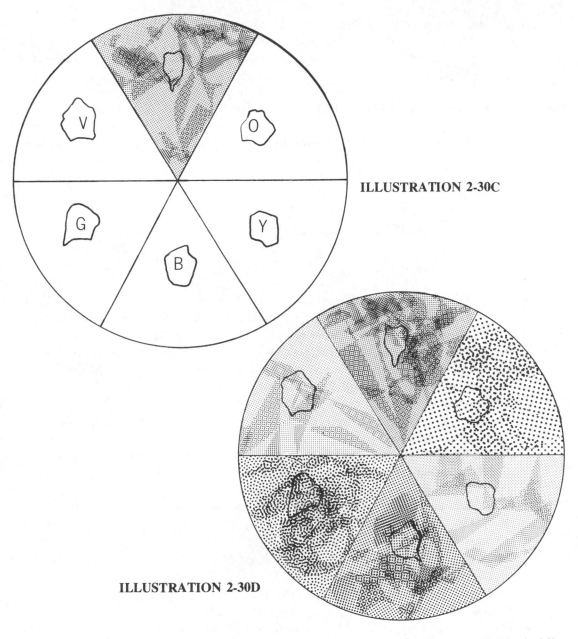

ILLUSTRATION 2-30C

ILLUSTRATION 2-30D

- Paste the bogus circle on the white construction paper. *Note:* Help individual children count how many different reds, oranges, yellows, etc. they have in their "Color Pie."

*Can You Imagine . . .*

Cut a long, green construction paper stem with leaves. Paste the end of the stem to the back of the "Color Pie." Tape the "color pie flowers" along the wall under the chalkboard.

Give a dull corner color by displaying several of the "Color Pies."

From magazines cut fruits or vegetables of different shades of each color. Group the items according to the colors on the "Color Pie." Paste the food items in the matching color sections in overlapping positions.

## COLOR PICTURE MATES (GRADES 3-4)

To create two separate compositions on a single working plane and link them together with color.

*You'll Need . . .*

Manila paper 12″ × 18″ • cool and warm shades of crayons.

*Procedures . . .*

- Play "What Goes with It?" Write the word *vases* on the chalkboard. Tell the children that you are thinking of something that goes with vases. Write the word *flowers* opposite *vases*. Continue with the game until there are at least ten to twelve word pairs. The following words may be used for children to respond to: clowns, brooms, balls, birds, trees, letters, tables, bells, buttons, hats, wheels, etc.
- Have children fold the manila paper in half widthwise.
- Select a pair of words from the list on the chalkboard.
- On the left half of the paper with crayon, draw a group of what the first word of the chosen pair says. (See Illustration 2-31A.)
- On the right side of the paper, draw several of what the other word of the pair says. (See Illustration 2-31B.) *Note:* Encourage children to draw more than two of an object and to use as much space as possible.
- Have children select four colors: three cool and one warm; or three warm and one cool. *Note:* The warm and cool colors may be listed on the chalkboard for the children's reference.
- Color the composition on the left with three of the four colors. (See Illustration 2-31C.) *Note:* Apply colors heavily.
- Substitute the fourth color for one of the three colors used on the left side and color the composition on the right as suggested in Illustration 2-31D.
- Choose one of the colors and lightly shade in the entire background of *both* compositions. (See Illustration 2-31E.)
- Blend a second color over the first background color.
- Display "Color Picture Mates." Have children look for the ones that use color more effectively to unite the two compositions.

*Can You Imagine . . .*

Paint over the surface of the composition with a very thin solution of water and yellow tempera paint.

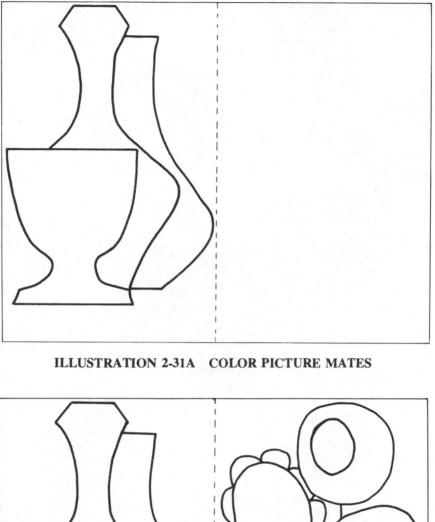

**ILLUSTRATION 2-31A   COLOR PICTURE MATES**

**ILLUSTRATION 2-31B**

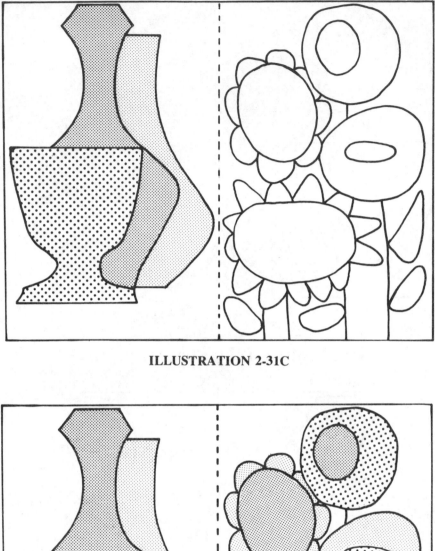

**ILLUSTRATION 2-31C**

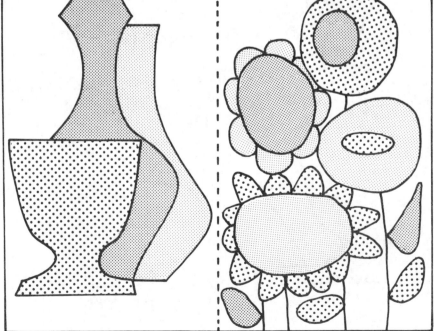

**ILLUSTRATION 2-31D**

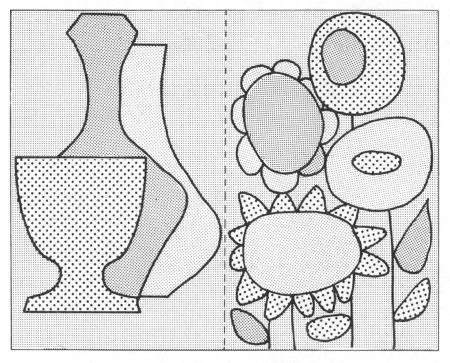

**ILLUSTRATION 2-31E**

Do a holiday "Color Picture Mate." Begin with the "What Goes with It?" game. For example, use the following Halloween words for children to respond to: *ghosts, witches, goblins, pumpkins, cats, bags,* etc.

Create a story panel using color to relate the frames to each other.

## ONE WARM AND ONE COOL (GRADES 5-6)

To experiment with and compare the effect of warm and cool colors on two identical compositions.

*You'll Need . . .*

Manila paper 9″ × 12″ (5 sheets per child) • scissors • newspaper • white construction paper 18″ × 24″ • black crayons • pencils • half sticks of colored chalk divided into two groups: reds, yellows, oranges; and greens, blues, violets (2 or 3 boxes of colored chalk will be needed so that each child can select 4 colors from each group) • 3″ × 5″ cards • paint cups • bucket of water • paper towels • spray fixative.

*Procedures . . .*

• Ask the children to name something that they see in the room (book, vase, plant, window, door, table, paper, pencil, board, clock, ball, etc.). List the items on the chalkboard.

- Have children fold some sheets of the manila paper in half widthwise and some in half lengthwise.
- Starting on the fold of one piece of manila paper, cut a half shape of one of the items listed on the board (Illustration 2-32).

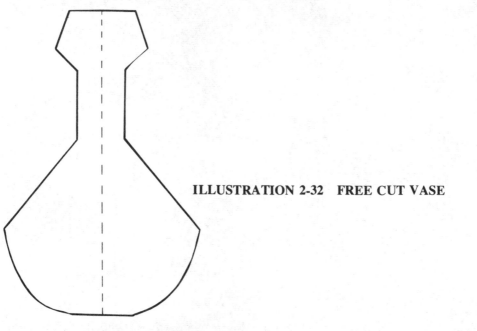

**ILLUSTRATION 2-32   FREE CUT VASE**

- From the other sheets of folded manila paper, cut half shapes of other items. *Note:* Children may select items from the board list or use other objects.
- Cover the desks with newspaper.
- Fold the white construction paper in half widthwise; then unfold.
- On the left half of the paper with black crayon, trace around one or more of the unfolded cutout objects as suggested in Illustration 2-33A. *Note:* All tracings should overlap in transparent positions so that the complete outline of each shape is visible. If only one cutout is used, then it can be traced several times in various overlapping positions. Be sure that crayoned lines are drawn heavily.
- Fold the completed drawing face down over the right half of the paper.
- Rub the back of the drawing with the side of a pencil so that lines of the crayon drawing appear on the right half of the paper. (See Illustration 2-33B.)
- With black crayon, trace over these lines on the right half and make them heavy.
- Select eight pieces of chalk: four warm colors and four cool.
- Accordian fold the 3″ × 5″ card, leaving about one-half inch space between folds to hold the chalk pieces when not in use. (See Illustration 2-34.)
- Put about a fourth of a cup of water in a paint cup.
- Dip the end of the chalk into water and color one of the compositions in four warm colors and the other in four cool colors. *Note:* Chalk should be moistened a little in order to smooth it onto the construction paper without dust forming. Too much water tends to make the chalk crumble. Place paper towel on desks for wiping chalky

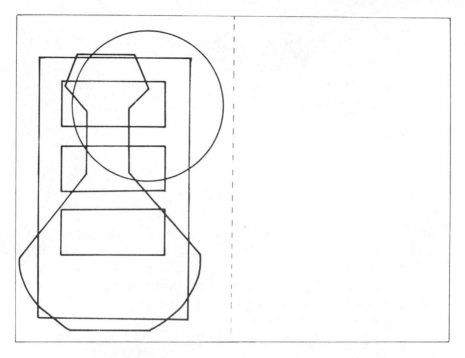

**ILLUSTRATION 2-33A   ARRANGEMENT OF SHAPES**

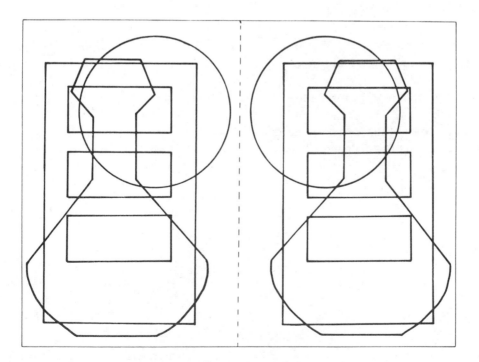

**ILLUSTRATION 2-33B**

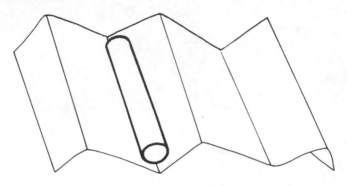

**ILLUSTRATION 2-34**
**CHALK TRAY**

fingers. Remind children to stay inside the crayoned lines and to take into consideration each shape that was formed where the traced shapes overlapped. After a space is colored and a line has to be crossed to begin coloring another space, change colors.

- Color in the background and all empty spaces of both completed compositions.
- After the pictures dry, spray them with the fixative to keep the chalk from rubbing off.
- Trace over all crayoned lines again with the black crayon to give the project a "finished" look.
- Discuss which colors seem to support each arrangement of shapes best.

*Can You Imagine . . .*

Fold the completed "One Warm and One Cool" so that the compositions are on the outside. Inside write an original birthday, get well, welcome back, or congratulatory greeting.

Illustrate a quiet, thoughtful scene (woods, library, river, cave, etc.) using all cool colors of chalk.

Cut out shapes of items that are normally illustrated with cool colors. Trace around the shapes on white construction paper. Use only warm colors of chalk to color this composition.

# CHAPTER 3

# VALUE AND INTENSITY

Art experiences in Chapters 1 and 2 provided opportunities to use and observe the primary colors (red, yellow, and blue), to combine them to create the secondary colors (orange, green, and violet) and to experiment with these six colors by grouping them in warm and cool categories. This chapter provides further exploration of color through experiments with value and intensity.

Children will use the knowledge gained in Chapters 1 and 2 as they experiment with value and intensity. They will begin to discover a whole new world of color and a new awareness of color. They will discover, for example, that all reds are not warm; violet containing more red than blue appears warm; green containing more yellow than blue is warm, not cool; orange reduced to a light value or tint by adding white is no longer bright; and yellow can be very cold under certain conditions.

This new awareness of color will stretch children's imaginations to a new dimension and will enable them to begin seeing aesthetically the most familiar objects from different vantage points as if for the first time.

## BEFORE YOU BEGIN

Play a color analysis game: Name something that children can see which has a color (sky, tree, building, etc.), or display an object (cloth, wastebasket, book, etc.). Ask questions about the color: Is it a primary or secondary color? If it is secondary, which of the primary colors does it seem to have the most? Is the color warm or cool? Is it a light color (*tint*) or a dark color (*shade*)? Is it bright or dull intensity?

Experiment with value. Cut from magazines eight swatches each of grays, reds, yellows, and blues (about 2″ × 2″). These eight samples of each color should range from very light to very dark. Tape the eight gray swatches in a group on the chalkboard. Near the group, tape a 2″ × 2″ piece of white construction paper. Ask a child to select one of the 2″ × 2″ gray patches that is closest in color to the white square. Tape this gray under the white patch. Ask which patch of gray in the group is the nearest in color to the one taped under the white square. Tape this second gray patch to the edge of the one under the white square.

**FIGURE 3-1    VALUE SCALE OF GRAYS**

Continue this procedure until all eight gray swatches (Figure 3-1) have been displayed so that each patch of gray is darker than the one above. Remove the square of white construction paper.

Explain that this display of light and dark grays in this order is called a *value scale*. Value of a color depends upon how much black or how much white is mixed with the color. Ask children to observe the first gray patch displayed on the board and explain that the lighter the value the more white the color has. Observe the gray swatch at the bottom and note that the darker the value the more black the color has. Ask children to note the arrangement of the gray swatches. Explain that a value scale is an arrangement of a group of light to dark variations of a color.

Ask the children to assist in arranging red, yellow, and blue value scales using magazine swatches of color. Display all four value scales along with a color wheel (see Chapter 1, ''Before You Begin'') for the class to use as reference during art sessions.

## CITY OF GRAY SHADES (GRADES K-2)

To experiment with gray tones in a gadget painting.

*You'll Need . . .*

Newspaper • 5 tablespoons or rulers for distributing paint • about 1 pint each of 3 values of gray paint (gray, light gray, off white) made from mixing different amounts of black and white tempera paint • cardboard 9″ × 12″ • cardboard strips 1″ × 2″ (4 to 6 per child) • bogus paper 20″ × 15″ • paper towels • sponge pieces 2″ to 1″ squares (3 per child) • small sticks of wood or halves of tongue depressors (3 per child) • white and black tempera paint.

*Procedures . . .*

- Cover the children's tables with newspaper.
- Put about one heaping tablespoon of each value of gray on each child's 9″ × 12″ cardboard which serves as the palette. (See Chapter 1, ''Before You Begin.'')*Note:* Use a clean tablespoon for each value. Leave space between the grays on the cardboard palette.
- Have children dip a wide edge of a cardboard strip into the gray tempera on the palette and starting near the top of the bogus paper, drag this edge of the strip in a vertical direction toward the bottom. (See Illustration 3-1A.) *Note:* Give children paper towels on which to put their painting tools when not in use.
- Dip a wide edge of another cardboard strip into the light gray tempera and brush the

**ILLUSTRATION 3-1A   CITY OF GRAY SHAPES**

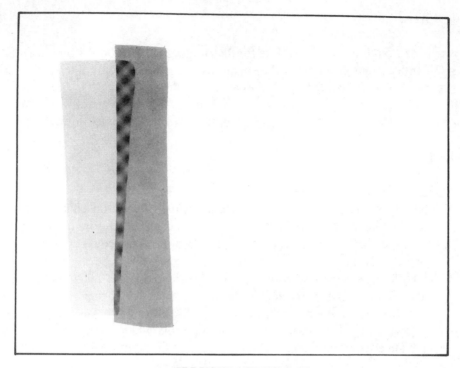

**ILLUSTRATION 3-1B**

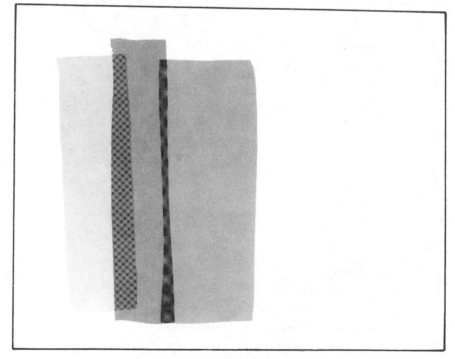

**ILLUSTRATION 3-1C**

paint on the bogus paper, overlapping previously applied gray. (See Illustration 3-1B.)

- Use another cardboard strip to apply the third value of gray, overlapping the previously applied value (Illustration 3-1C).
- Continue to apply alternately the three values of gray until the bogus paper is almost covered. *Note:* It is *not* important for all painted areas to be straight and in exact vertical positions. (See Illustration 3-1D.) Emphasize:
  —Applying each value of gray independently by using a clean cardboard strip for each shade. (However, once a strip has been used to apply a value, it can be reused with that same value.)
  —Overlapping the grays.
  —Dragging the wide edge of a cardboard strip on the bogus so that painted shapes are achieved rather than drawn lines.
- Ask children what these shapes of gray values remind them of. *Note:* Accept all responses.
- Have children dip a cardboard strip into the gray tempera and paint windows and doors on the gray shapes. (See Illustration 3-1E.)
- Ask children to name other things beside buildings that they usually see on city streets, such as mailboxes, stop signs, telephone poles, etc.
- Paint gray street objects in the compositions. (See Illustration 3-1F.)
- Use the sponges and pieces of wood to experiment with painting other shapes and details of grays in the composition. (See Illustration 3-1G.) *Note:* Remind children

**ILLUSTRATION 3-1D**

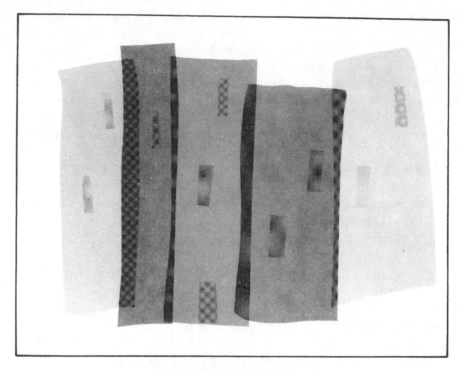

**ILLUSTRATION 3-1E**

**ILLUSTRATION 3-1F**

**ILLUSTRATION 3-1G**

that once a sponge or wood piece is dipped in one value of gray paint, it should be used again only when they want to paint with that same value.

- Give children about ½ teaspoon of black and white tempera paint on their palettes. *Note:* Issuing just a small amount of black and white paint will help prevent children from turning their ''city'' into a total dark or white composition.
- Add touches of black and white paint to different parts of objects in the picture. For example, make the edges of buildings white, paint undersides of branches black, etc.

*Can You Imagine . . .*

Add red, yellow and orange crayon to various areas of the painting.

Cut out magazine pictures (gray or black and white only) of children and animals. Paste them on the painting.

Cut out a magazine or poster picture of an airplane. Paste it on the bogus paper. Children paint a background sky and clouds of gray on the bogus.

## BLOTTO FACES IN GRAYS (GRADES 3-4)

To create a composition of faces by pressing and blotting overlapping values of gray.

*You'll Need . . .*

Newspaper • cardboard 9″ × 12″ • 5 tablespoons or rulers for distributing paint • about 1 pint each of 5 values of thick gray paint made by mixing different amounts of black and white tempera paint • white construction paper 12″ × 18″ • cardboard strips 1″ × 2″ (8 per child) • paper towels • colored felt markers.

### *Procedures . . .*

- Cover the desks with newspaper.
- On each child's cardboard which serves as the paint palette, put about 1 tablespoon each of the five gray values. *Note:* If more paint is needed for this procedure, it is not necessary to mix values that are identical to those previously obtained. Though a child will have five gray values, each value does not have to be the same as another child's.
- Have children fold the construction paper in half lengthwise.
- With a cardboard strip, scoop up about half of one gray value of paint and place it on the lower half of the construction paper. (See Illustration 3-2A.) *Note:* Remind children to use a clean cardboard strip for scooping each value. Place used strips on the paper towel for painting with the same color later.
- In like manner, put half of each of the other four grays on the bottom half of the construction paper, but do not allow them to touch each other. (See Illustration 3-2B.) *Note:* There is no special arrangement required for distributing the five values of color on the paper, but there should be space left around each gray.
- On each gray value of paint on the construction paper, with cardboard strips paint on facial features using from the palette grays that are darker or lighter. (See Illustration 3-2C.)

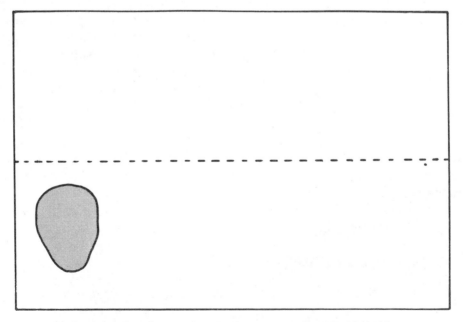

**ILLUSTRATION 3-2A BLOTTO FACES IN GRAYS**

- Carefully fold the top half of the paper over the painted faces.
- Press down firmly on the top half to spread and blot the paint so that facsimiles of faces on the bottom half appear on the underside of the top half of the paper.
- Lift the top half of the paper (Illustration 3-2D) and allow both halves to dry.

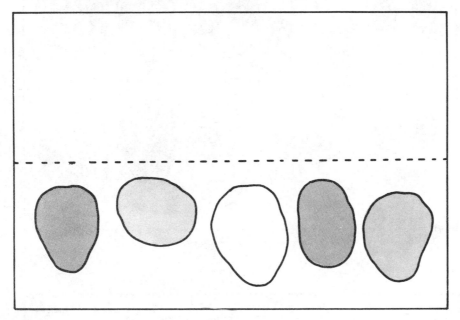

**ILLUSTRATION 3-2B**

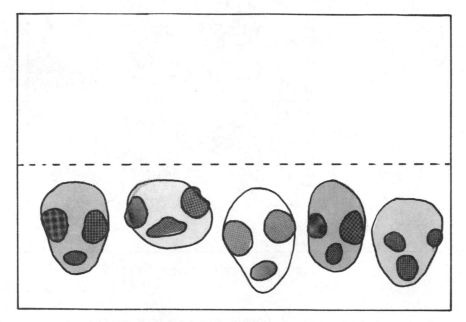

**ILLUSTRATION 3-2C**

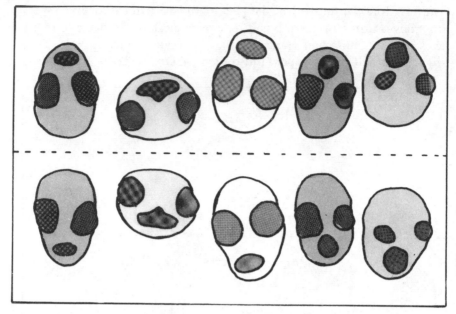

**ILLUSTRATION 3-2D**

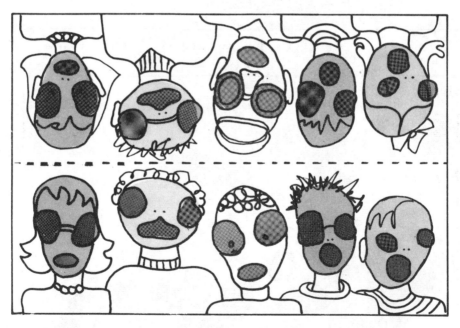

**ILLUSTRATION 3-2E**

- For added emphasis use the colored markers to draw lines around faces and features and to add necks, hair, shoulders, etc. (See Illustration 3-2E.)
- Cut the construction paper on the fold. Mount and display the compositions.

*Can You Imagine . . .*

Place both compositions side by side. Compare and discuss line emphasis and gray values of each composition. Determine which composition is stronger in use of values.

Use "Blotto Faces in Grays" for wall decorations during Halloween.

Cut out the faces and paste in overlapping positions on a rectangular piece of bright colored construction paper.

## ANIMAL SILHOUETTES IN GRAYS (GRADES 5-6)

To create and observe the effect of a composition of gray values in repetition on a black background.

*You'll Need . . .*

A variety of animal pictures ● manila paper 9″ × 12″ ● pencils ● scissors ● stencil paper (wax coated paper) or brown kraft paper 5″ × 7″ ● cardboard 6″ × 9″ ● 3 tablespoons ● about 1 pint each of 3 values of gray paint made by mixing different amounts of black and white tempera paint ● newspaper ● black construction paper 18″ × 18″ ● sponge pieces 1½″ × 1″ (4 per child) ● paper towels.

*Procedures . . .*

- Display the animal pictures. Discuss differences in animal shapes, legs, necks, ears, heads, and tails.
- Have children divide the manila paper into fourths by folding it in half lengthwise and widthwise.
- Make a pencilled outlined drawing or silhouette of a different animal shape (Illustration 3-3) in each box on the paper.
- Cut out the favorite animal silhouette.
- Place the cutout animal silhouette in the center of the stencil paper and trace around the shape with a pencil.
- With the point of the scissors, punch a hole in the center of the traced shape and carefully cut out the traced shape. (See Illustration 3-4A.) *Note:* Explain to the class that this paper with the hole shaped like an animal is called a *stencil*. While the stencils are being made, give each child a cardboard palette containing about a tablespoon each of the three gray values of tempera paint.
- Cover the desks with newspaper.
- Place the animal stencil on the black paper.
- Dip the end of a sponge in the light gray paint and dab the paint lightly through the cutout area of the stencil paper onto the construction paper (Illustration 3-4B) while holding the stencil steady with one hand.
- Completely cover the cutout area with paint and then carefully lift the stencil. *Note:* Have paper towels available for painting tools when not in use.
- On the construction paper, make more stencilled animal shapes, using the three

**ILLUSTRATION 3-3   OUTLINED ANIMAL SHAPES**

**ILLUSTRATION 3-4A   STENCILING AN ANIMAL**

values of gray to create an arrangement of gray animal silhouettes. (See Illustration 3-4C.) *Note:* For a successful stenciling experience, remind children to:
   —Hold the stencil steady.
   —Dab from the outer edge of the hole toward the center to prevent paint from going under the stencil and spoiling the outline.
   —Use a different sponge for each color value of paint.

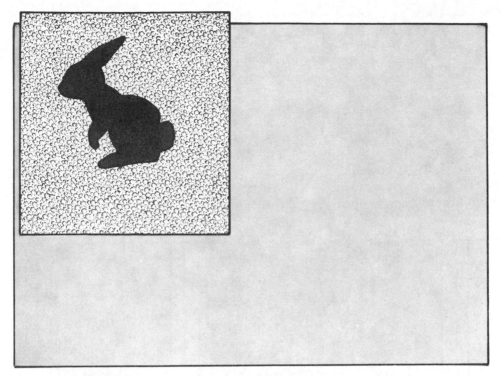

**ILLUSTRATION 3-4B**

**ILLUSTRATION 3-4C**

—Use a paper towel to clean any paint smudges on back of the stencil.

—Lift the stencil in a vertical manner to prevent smearing.

—Let a silhouette dry if the stencil must cover or touch it when making another stencilled shape.

*Can You Imagine . . .*

Use completed arrangements of ''Animal Silhouettes'' for book covers.

Use white tempera and cardboard to print vertical and horizontal lines between animal shapes. (See Illustration 3-5.)

Create a parade of animals. On a 9″ wide paper strip, each child makes one stencil of an animal. Add construction paper grass, and trees to the strip. Use in panels for a room border.

**ILLUSTRATION 3-5   LINEAR AND ANIMAL PATTERNS**

## COLOR CHARADE (GRADES K-2)

To create a one-color composition.

*You'll Need . . .*

Three colors (preferably red, yellow, and blue) of cellophane paper 1″ × 3″ (1 color of each per child) • red, yellow, blue, green, orange, and violet construction paper 12″ × 24″ (1 color of each child's choice) ● collection of different values of red, yellow, blue, violet, green, and orange construction paper 4½" × 6", cloth scraps (solid colors), and string ● scissors ● magazines ● paste ● paste dabbers or brushes.

*Procedures . . .*

- Ask children to imagine what the world would look like if they wore colored glasses. To help them explore this idea, have them experiment looking through the different colors of cellophane at objects and people in the room and through the window. Ask questions similar to the following: Is everything the same red? What colors make the day appear warm? Cool? What color makes an object appear darker green? What happens to a yellow object when you look at it through another color? What color seems to make things shine?
- Have children each select a color of 12" × 24" construction paper. *Note:* Explain that the color chosen represents the color of eyeglasses that the child will pretend to be looking through.
- From the collection of the small pieces of construction paper, cloth scraps, and string, have children choose four or five of the items that are of the color, but not necessarily same in value, of the 12" × 24" paper selected.
- Ask children to cut from their selected materials shapes of objects for a street setting (Illustration 3-6).

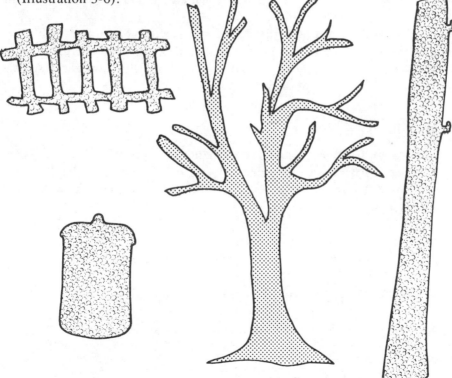

**ILLUSTRATION 3-6 STREET OBJECTS CREATED FROM DIFFERENT MEDIA**

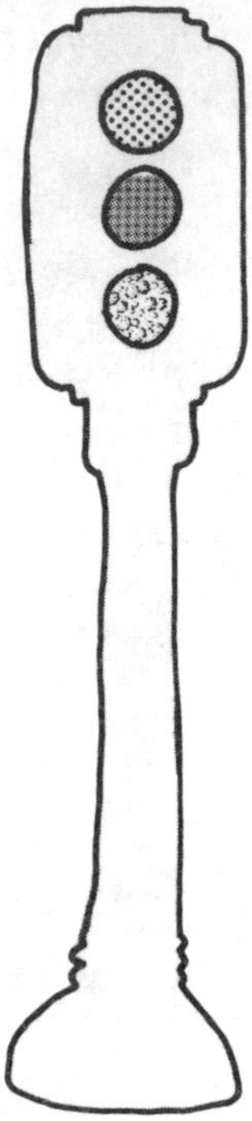

**ILLUSTRATION 3-7   CUTOUT MAGAZINE OBJECTS**

- Cut out magazine objects (Illustration 3-7) that are the same color as the construction paper.
- Add shapes cut from magazine patches of the selected color. *Note:* A blue building could be shaped from a large patch of blue from a magazine picture.
- Arrange and paste all pictures and shapes on the construction paper so that some items overlap. (See Illustration 3-8.)

*Can You Imagine . . .*

Cover each "Color Charade" with a primary color of cellophane. If a child's project is red, yellow, or blue, cover it with the same color of cellophane. If a child's project is a secondary color, cover it with cellophane of one of the colors that makes up that color. For example, cover a green "Color Charade" with yellow or blue.

Choose a secondary color of construction paper. For the street scene, select materials of a color that makes up the selected secondary color.

With crayon the color of the selected construction paper, color the background.

## COLOR VALUES AND PAPER DOLLS (GRADES 3-4)

To mix and use five values of a color in creating a composition.

*You'll Need . . .*

Manila paper 6″ × 9″ (2 sheets per child) • scissors • red, yellow, and blue construction

**ILLUSTRATION 3-8 COLOR CHARADE**

paper 12″ × 18″ (1 sheet of each child's choice) • red, yellow, and blue crayons (1 piece of the same color as the color of paper selected) • newspaper • cardboard 9″ × 12″ • 5 tablespoons or rulers for distributing paint • 2 pints each of red, yellow, blue, white, and black tempera paint • cardboard strips 1″ × 2″ (8 per child) • paper towels.

*Procedures . . .*

- Have children fold the manila paper in half lengthwise.
- On the fold, cut out one half of a doll shape as suggested in Illustration 3-9. *Note:* Children may use both sheets of manila paper to experiment with cutting a doll shape.
- Have children select a piece of construction paper and place it in a horizontal position on the desk.
- Place the unfolded doll shape on the left side of the construction paper and trace around the doll, using crayon that is the color of the paper.
- Move the figure to the right so that it is close to but does not overlap the first tracing and trace around the doll again.
- Continue to move and trace the figure until a row of paper dolls extends across the paper as suggested in Illustration 3-10.
- Cover the desks with newspaper.

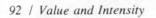

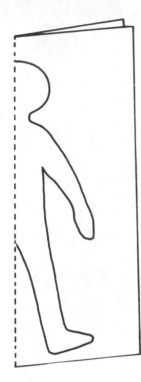

**ILLUSTRATION 3-9
DOLL FIGURE**

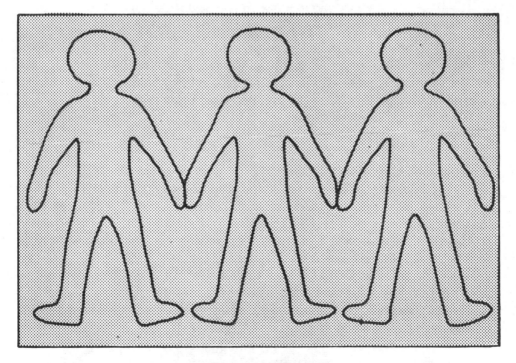

**ILLUSTRATION 3-10
TRACED FIGURES**

- On each child's cardboard palette, place five separate tablespoons of paint that is the same color as the construction paper, and one tablespoon each of white and black paint as suggested in Illustration 3-11.

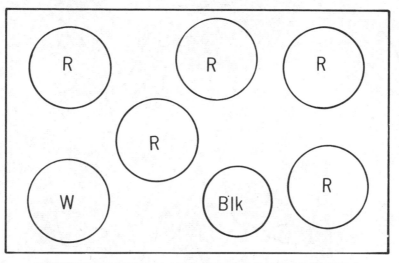

**ILLUSTRATION 3-11   PREPARED PAINT PALETTE**

- With a cardboard strip, scoop up half of the white paint and mix it with one of the "cakes" of color on the palette to make it a lighter value. *Note:* Remind children to mix the paint carefully in that one spot so that the color doesn't spread. Put used cardboard paint strips on a paper towel and save for later use.
- With a clean cardboard strip, mix half of the remaining white paint with a second "cake" of color to make a value that is not as light as the previous one.
- Using clean cardboard strips, mix half of the black paint with a third "cake" of color and the remaining black with a fourth "cake" of color to create two different values.
- Using the original cardboard strip for each of the values, paint rectangles of different color values around the paper doll figures. (See Illustration 3-12.) *Note:* Remind children to use each value in several places on the background. Some areas may remain unpainted.
- With a clean cardboard strip, use the remaining unmixed "cake" of color to paint the row of paper dolls.
- When the paint is completely dry, with the crayon draw heavy lines between the various rectangles and around the paper dolls.

*Can You Imagine . . .*

To emphasize the range of color values, display all red "Color Values and Paper Dolls" together on one wall of the room. On another wall display all yellow projects, and on a third wall exhibit all blue projects. Encourage children to try to count the different values of a color.

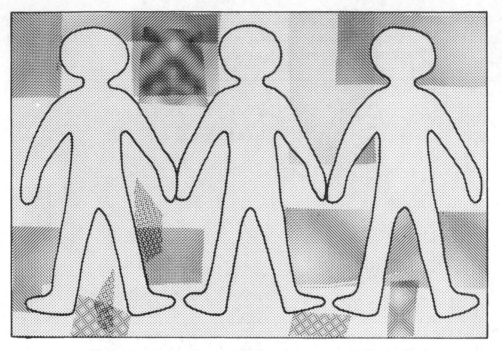

**ILLUSTRATION 3-12   COLOR VALUES AND PAPER DOLLS**

Paint some areas of the construction paper with rectangles of values of a different color. Cut out balloon shapes from magazine swatches of values of that color. Paste balloon shapes on the construction paper after rectangles dry. With paste attach end of a piece of string or yarn to each balloon shape. Paste opposite ends of string pieces together on the paper near the bottom of the composition.

Cut magazine swatches of values of a color and paste on 9″ × 12″ construction paper of the same color. From another sheet of construction paper of the same color but of a different value, free cut several shapes of an item that usually is associated with that color. For example, if yellow is the basic color, banana, pear, school bus, or duck shapes may be cut. Paste the shapes in a row on top of the magazine swatches.

## TEXTURED CHECKERBOARD OF VALUES (GRADES 5-6)

To experience mixing a value scale and using it in composition.

*You'll Need . . .*

Newspaper • red, yellow, and blue construction paper 9″ × 9″ (1 color per child's choice) • cardboard 9″ × 12″ • 5 tablespoons or rulers for distributing paint • 2 pints each of red, yellow, blue, black, and white tempera paint mixed to the consistency of mustard (see Chapter 1, ''Before You Begin'') • cardboard strips 1″ × 2″ (14 per child) • paper towels.

*Procedures . . .*

- Review the meaning of *color value*. (See "Before You Begin.") Ask the class what would be the lightest value of red. Tell them the easiest way to make this very light pink is to mix a "tiny bit" of red paint with a large amount of white paint. Ask children how they would make a dark value of red.
- Cover desks with newspaper.
- Have children each select a piece of construction paper.
- Fold the paper into *sixteen* square spaces by folding in half twice lengthwise and then twice widthwise.
- On three separate areas of the cardboard palette, place about two tablespoons of tempera paint of the same color as the construction paper, and in two other areas put two tablespoons each of white and black tempera paint. For example, see Illustration 3-13.

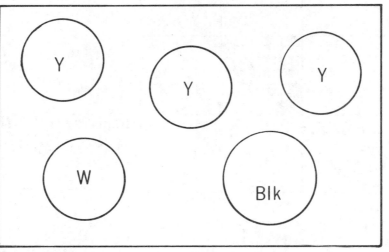

**ILLUSTRATION 3-13   PREPARED PAINT PALETTE**

- With a cardboard strip, paint one space of the folded construction paper with the primary color. *Note:* Place used cardboard paint strips on a paper towel and save for later use.
- With a clean cardboard strip, scoop up a small amount of white paint from the palette and place it in one space of the construction paper.
- With a clean cardboard strip, scoop up about a drop of the primary color from the palette and mix it with the white paint in the space on the construction paper. *Note:* Remind children to spread the color so that it covers the entire space and stays within the borders created by the folds surrounding the space.
- Continue to mix different amounts of the primary color of paint with white or black paint to create a different value of the primary color for each of the *thirteen* additional spaces. *Note:* The black and white paint are not to be mixed together. Remind children that one space is to be left unpainted. Explain that when they have finished,

they will have sixteen spaces with different values: one space that is the exact color of the construction paper, one space that is painted with the primary color of paint, and fourteen spaces that are painted with values of the color.

- After the painted spaces dry, use an edge of a cardboard strip dipped in the primary color to make patterns or designs in several of the spaces as suggested in Illustration 3-14.

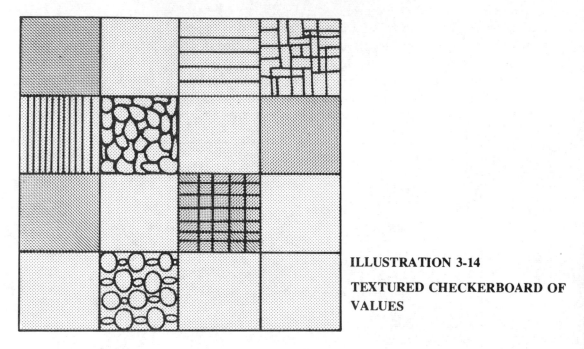

**ILLUSTRATION 3-14**

**TEXTURED CHECKERBOARD OF VALUES**

- Have children study the compositions and compare the brightness and the dullness of the primary color and its values.

*Can You Imagine . . .*

Mount the checkerboard of values on a white board for display and study.

Create a checkerboard of values for a primary color not selected for the project. For the various values, use not only tempera paint but also colored construction (or wrapping) paper, magazine color patches, and cloth swatches.

Do a checkerboard of values for each of the secondary colors.

## AN ANIMALFISHBIRDBUG (GRADES K-2)

To use bright and dull colors in isolated groupings.

*You'll Need . . .*

Several color pictures of various insects, animals, birds, and fish; including a ladybug, beetle, grasshopper, butterfly, elephant, tiger, giraffe, robin, bluejay, cardinal • film or filmstrip on insects, animals, birds, and fish if possible • manila paper 9″ × 12″ • crayons • gray bogus paper 10″ × 10″ • collection of bright and dull colors of cloth scraps (corduroy, satin, velvet, cotton denim, wool, etc.) and paper scraps (foil, gift wrapping paper, etc.) 2″ × 2″, ribbon scraps and yarn pieces (3 or 4 of a variety of items per child) • scissors • paste • paste brushes or dabbers.

*Procedures . . .*

- Use the filmstrips, films, and/or pictures to discuss likenesses and differences in animals, birds, fish, and insects. Point out characteristics of each group; for example, fur, feathers, scales, number of legs, etc.
- Have children make simple drawings of a fish, animal, bird, and insect on the manila paper with crayons. *Note:* Do not dwell on perfecting drawings. This step is merely to establish basic characteristics of these four creatures.
- Ask children to close their eyes and try to imagine a creature you describe. Say the following slowly:

    > *Once there was a strange insect. It had six legs that looked like bird legs. It had a giraffe neck and a fish head. This strange insect had bird wings and its body was covered with scales.*

- Ask children to open their eyes and on back of the manila paper, draw with crayon what they imagine this creature looked like, for example, see Illustration 3-15. *Note:* While children are drawing, repeat the general description of the creature but add emphasis such as "*six* bird legs"; "a neck as *long* as a giraffe."
- On the bogus square with crayon, have children create another bug or insect. *Note:* Review different features or characteristics of animals, birds, fish, and insects in the displayed pictures so that the children will be encouraged to draw an insect different from the one you described. You may suggest characteristics to combine similar to those suggested in Illustration 3-16.
- Trace over the drawing to make crayon lines thick and heavy.
- Have children select from the collection of scraps either all dull or all bright colors for their "animalfishbirdbugs." *Note:* From the collection of scraps, show and identify samples of bright and dull colors. (See "Before You Begin.")
- Cut and tear scraps into smaller pieces and paste on the insect. *Note:* Scraps may overlap.
- Discuss places in which the children's creatures might be found, for example, near water, on land, in the woods, in tall grass, among leaves. Encourage children to think of ways to illustrate places for their "animalfishbirdbug." Explain that if they made their creatures of dull colors, they must use bright colors for the place shapes. Conversely, if the insects were made with bright colors, the place shapes must be dull colors.
- Have children select and cut or tear place shapes from either dull or bright colored scraps and paste them around the insect. (See Illustration 3-17.) *Note:* Encourage overlapping of shapes.

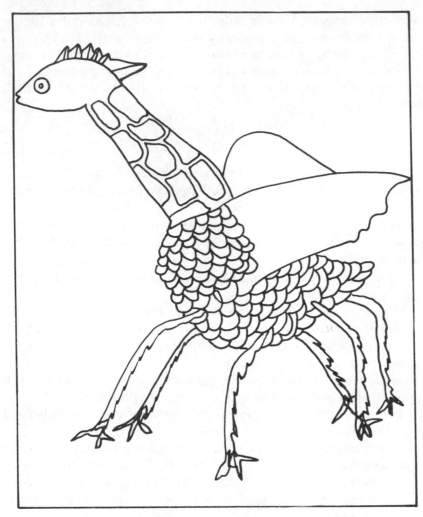

**ILLUSTRATION 3-15   IMAGINED CREATURE**

**ILLUSTRATION 3-16   DIFFERENT IMAGINED CREATURES**

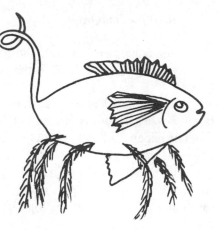

**ILLUSTRATION 3-16   DIFFERENT IMAGINED
CREATURES (CONTINUED)**

**ILLUSTRATION 3-17
ANIMALFISHBIRDBUG
WITH BACKGROUND**

*Can You Imagine . . .*

Create another "animalfishbirdbug" of color intensity opposite from the color used for the insect in the project. Use the opposite intensity of colors for the place environmental shapes.

Tear and cut shapes from scraps of dull colors and paste in overlapping positions on the bogus square until it is covered. Tear or cut an animal shape from a scrap of bright colored cloth or paper. Paste the animal shape on the dull scraps, leaving at least two inches from the edges of the bogus.

Give each child a 4" or 5" square of bogus paper. Ask half the class to cover their squares with cloth and paper scraps of bright colors and the other half to do the same using dull colors. Mix all squares together and show one at a time for children to identify as dull colors or bright colors.

## PEOPLE FIGURES DRESSED IN COMPLEMENTS (GRADES 3-4)

To experiment with color complements in a composition.

*You'll Need . . .*

Pencils • white practice cards 3" × 7" • newspaper • scissors • a color wheel (see Chapter 1, "Before You Begin") • red, yellow, blue, green, orange, and violet construction paper 4½" × 3" • red, yellow, blue, orange, green, and violet yarn 4" lengths • paste • paste brushes or dabbers • red, yellow, blue, orange, and violet construction paper 6" × 9".

*Procedures . . .*

- With a pencil, have children trace around the practice card on the newspaper to make five separate rectangular shapes.
- Cut out the rectangular shapes and fold each in half lengthwise.
- Starting on the fold, free cut half of a people figure from each paper rectangle as suggested in Illustration 3-18. *Note:* Encourage children to cut the figure as tall as possible.
- Display the color wheel. Explain that color complements are colors opposite each other on the color wheel. Ask the class to examine the color wheel and identify each group of complements: red and green, orange and blue, yellow and violet.
- On their desks, have children make three groups of the 4½" × 3" pieces of construction paper by placing the color complements together.
- Group the yarn pieces also according to color complements.
- From the small construction paper pieces in one group on the desk, cut clothes for any one of the people figures.
- Dress the figure by pasting on the clothes. (See Illustration 3-19A.) *Note:* Encourage children to add paper details to the clothes: button shapes, collars, ties, patterns, etc. Encourage them to consider the color pairs when designing the clothes and to think about clothes for different occasions.

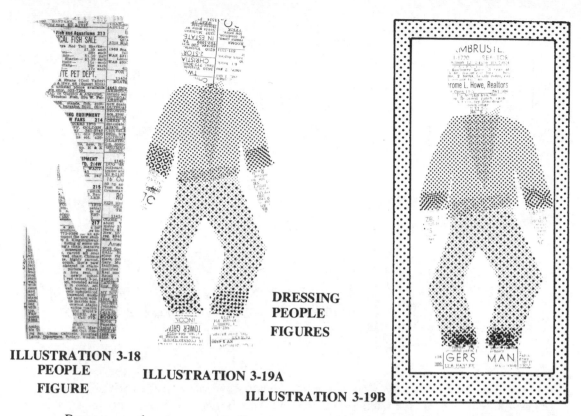

**ILLUSTRATION 3-18
PEOPLE
FIGURE**

**ILLUSTRATION 3-19A**

**DRESSING
PEOPLE
FIGURES**

**ILLUSTRATION 3-19B**

- Dress any other two people figures—one in clothes cut from another group of the complementary colors and the other figure in clothes cut from the remaining group.
- Paste on matching colors of yarn for hair and for other details on clothes of the three dressed figures.
- Paste each dressed people figure on a practice card.
- Paste each card on a 6″ × 9″ piece of construction paper of one of the color complements used in the figure's costume. (See Illustration 3-19B.)

*Can You Imagine . . .*

Display the newspaper figures in complementary color groupings.

Use as special program covers or souvenirs for parents at open house.

Paste a cardboard stand on back of each mounted people figure and use as place cards. (See Illustration 3-20.)

## A TRIPTYCH OF COMPLEMENTS (GRADES 5-6)

To experience the effect of mixing a color with its complement in a composition.

*You'll Need . . .*

One or more reproductions of triptych paintings, for example: *The Prado Madrid* ,

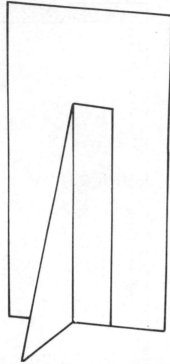

**ILLUSTRATION 3-20**
**CARDBOARD STAND FOR PEOPLE FIGURES**

Lorenzetti's *The Birth of the Virgin* ● white construction paper 12″ × 18″ ● pencils ● 12″ rulers ● a color wheel (see Chapter 1, ''Before You Begin'') ● 6 tablespoons or rulers for distributing paint ● 2 pints each of red, yellow, blue, orange, green, and violet tempera paint each mixed well with ⅓ cup of white tempera to soften each color and mixed to the consistency of mustard ● waxed paper 9″ × 12″ ● cardboard 9″ × 12″ ● stapler and staples ● cardboard strips 1″ × 2″ ● paper towels.

*Procedures . . .*

- Display one or more prints of a triptych painting. Encourage children to comment on them. Identify the prints as a triptych and write the word *triptych* on the chalkboard. Ask a child to read a dictionary definition of *triptych* to the class. Discuss the definition. Include the words *hinged* and *panel* in the discussion.
- Have children fold the construction paper widthwise into three equal panels.
- With pencil and ruler draw a border inside each panel leaving about an inch on all four sides. (See Illustration 3-21A.)
- On the panels, lightly illustrate with pencil three scenes from a favorite library book as suggested in Illustration 3-21B. *Note:* Avoid small details in the illustration; include only objects and background necessary to portray the story with simple pictures.
- Display the color wheel. *Note:* Explain that colors opposite each other such as *red* and *green* on the color wheel are called *color complements*. A color can be dulled by mixing it with its complement. For example, a red can be of a high intensity which

**ILLUSTRATION 3-21A**

**ILLUSTRATION 3-21B**
**PENCIL DRAWINGS FOR TRIPTYCH**

means that red is bright. When a little green is mixed with a bright red, the intensity is lowered or the red is dulled. Have children name the other color complements (yellow and violet, orange and blue).

- To demonstrate the effect of a color mixed with its complement, mix ¼ tablespoon of green tempera paint with one tablespoon of red. Encourage children to discuss the change in the red.
- Add and mix another ¼ tablespoon of green paint to the dull red mixture. Ask the class to note that as more green is added the intensity of red is lowered and the red become duller.
- Have children place the waxed paper on top of the cardboard so that both are in horizontal positions and staple them together at the four corners.
- On this waxed paint palette place three separate tablespoons each of a color and of its complement (Illustration 3-22) selected for use in the triptych.

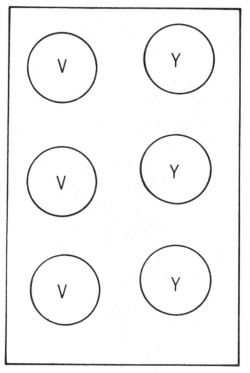

**ILLUSTRATION 3-22**
**PREPARED PAINT PALETTE**

- On different clean areas of the waxed palette, using cardboard strips, create at least four lower intensities of each of the two colors by mixing varied amounts of each color with its complement. *Note:* Remind children to put their used cardboard strips on a paper towel to save for using again with the same intensities of color.
- Using a clean cardboard strip, paint some areas of the left panel of the white construction paper with the unmixed primary color and paint other areas with lower intensities of this color.
- Using both unmixed color complements from the palette, paint some areas of the second panel and paint other areas of the same panel with lower intensities of both

colors. *Note:* The panels relate to each other through color and each still maintains its own color grouping.

- Paint some areas of the panel on the right using the unmixed secondary color and paint other areas of the same panel using lower intensities of this color. (See Illustration 3-23.)

**ILLUSTRATION 3-23   A TRIPTYCH OF COMPLEMENTS**

*Can You Imagine . . .*

Fold a 1″ wide section along the 12″ side of 8″ × 12″ cardboard. Paste the section on the back of the center panel of the triptych. Stand the triptych on the library table.

Create special holiday triptychs using dull and bright bits of cloth and other media instead of paint.

Fold the construction paper into thirds and draw a pencilled border inside each panel. Fill the first panel on the left with overlapping wide vertical or horizontal paint strokes of the unmixed primary color and strokes of lower intensities of this color. In the center panel, fill with overlapping wide vertical or horizontal paint strokes of the unmixed color complements and strokes of lower intensities of both colors. Fill the right panel with overlapping wide vertical or horizontal paint strokes of the unmixed secondary color and strokes of lower intensities of this color.

# CHAPTER 4

# LINE EXPERIMENTS

This chapter is designed to create a lasting awareness of the importance and power of the line. A line can divide, multiply, surround, join, and guide; a line is visible and can be imagined. (See Figure 4-1.) The line is used to express emotions and moods, and to represent ideas graphically.

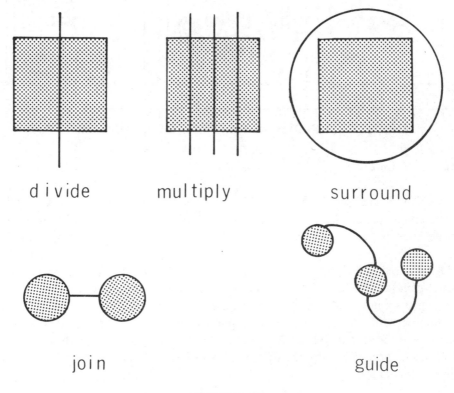

divide      multiply      surround

join      guide

**FIGURE 4-1**

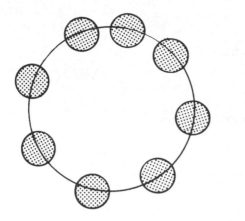
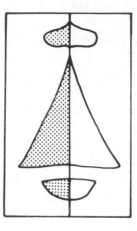

visible

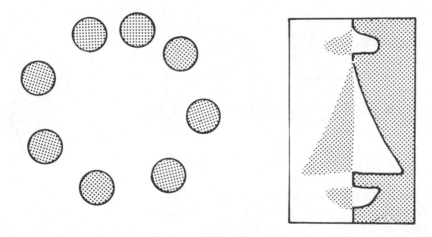

imaginary

**FIGURE 4-1 (CONTINUED)**

Experiments with line repetition using a variety of media are suggested. Through these projects children will develop the ability to see the line singularly and in repetition, and to see the line in relation to space and shape. To become more aware of the line is to strengthen the ability to use line effectively in creating stronger compositions.

## BEFORE YOU BEGIN

Carry out the following discussion as you draw these lines on the chalkboard:
Have you ever thought about a line? Just an ordinary line?

A vertical line?

A horizontal line?   ———

Did you know that a line gives information?

This line says, "Stand straight!"

This line may tell that someone is a little nervous.

Give the children crayon and 9″ × 12″ manila paper. Have them show the following. (Their lines do not have to match the examples given here.)

A line that is sleeping.   ———

A drooping line.

A leaning line

and an angry line.

A line that shows high and low.

On the board, illustrate these lines that tell about water:

ripples                    rain                    waves                    waterfall

Have the children draw other lines that represent water.

Explain to the children that if a line keeps on going, eventually it might form a shape. The shape may be formed with a straight line or with a curved line or with a line that is sometimes straight and sometimes curved. Then draw these shapes, explaining that they are continuous line shapes that have no beginning and no ending that can be seen. Ask the children to describe the line used to form each shape.

straight line

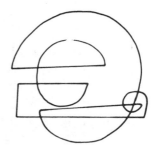

curved line

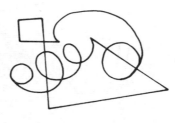

combination of straight and curved lines

Have the children experiment with making other line shapes.

## A CONTINUOUS LINE OF THINGS (GRADES K-2)

To use a continuous line to create a free, uncluttered arrangement of shapes.

*You'll Need . . .*

Crayons • white drawing paper 12″ × 18″ • pastel muslin or cotton 12″ × 12″ • colored cloth scraps 2″ × 2″ (3 or 4 per child) • paste • paste dabbers or brushes • scissors • 8 pieces of kraft paper 14″ × 14″ • an iron.

*Procedures . . .*

- Help children understand the meaning of the word *continuous* by drawing on the chalkboard a ball without lifting the chalk. Continue with drawings of a basket, boat, and clown. (See Illustration 4-1.)
- With crayon have children make a continuous line drawing of a ball on the paper. *Note:* To encourage enthusiastic participation, say: "Make a ball with designs on it. Do not begin until I saw 'Draw!' Keep drawing and do not lift your crayon from the paper until I say, 'Stop!'"

**ILLUSTRATION 4-1 DEMONSTRATIONS OF CONTINUOUS LINE DRAWINGS**

- Have children try the continuous ball drawing several times. *Note:* Remind them not to lift their crayon from the paper while drawing a ball.
- Have children draw a flower, bird, and boat. *Note:* Allow only about four seconds for any drawing of an item. Children may draw an object as many times as they wish, using both sides of the paper.
- Have children look at each of their drawings and select the one they like best.
- On the muslin or cotton square, with crayon make several continuous line *connected* drawings of the selected object. *Note:* Ask children to continue drawing the object without lifting the crayon from the cloth until the cloth is covered (Illustration 4-2A). It helps to pretend that the crayon is stuck to the cloth. If some children have problems with the cloth slipping as they draw, tape it to the desk with masking tape.
- Trace over all lines to make them thick and dark.
- Arrange and paste cloth scraps in different areas to add color. (See Illustration 4-2B.) *Note:* Scraps may be cut and used for designs on the ball, eyes on the birds, flower centers, boat sails, etc.

**ILLUSTRATION 4-2A    A CONTINUOUS LINE DRAWING OF THINGS**

**ILLUSTRATION 4-2B**

- Place the cloth between double layers of kraft paper and press with a warm iron. *Note:* Ironing will melt the crayoned lines.

*Can You Imagine . . .*

Use the cloths as placemats to brighten the table at a luncheon for mothers.

Paste compositions on white illustrator's board and hang on walls in columns of threes.

Do the drawing on burlap. On the lines of the drawings, press yarn soaked in liquid starch concentrate onto the burlap. *Note:* Place waxed paper under the burlap to protect desk tops. Keep fingers wet with starch to prevent them from pulling the yarn off the burlap.

## INK LINES (GRADES 3-4)

To experiment with recording line design by using cardboard and ink creatively.

*You'll Need . . .*

Newspaper • scissors • cardboard 8-1/2″ × 11″ or 9″ × 12″ • black drawing ink (2 tablespoonful per child) • jar lids for ink containers • gray bogus paper 15″ × 20″ or manila drawing paper 12″ × 18″ • paper towels • crayons (2 colors of each child's choice).

*Procedures . . .*

- Cover desks with newspaper.
- Have children cut the cardboard into 2″ lengths of various widths and alter the ends of some strips with scissors. (See Illustration 4-3.)

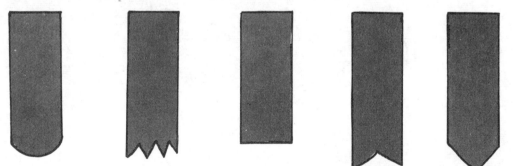

**ILLUSTRATION 4-3   A VARIETY OF CARDBOARD PAINT STICKS**

- Dip the ends of the cardboard pieces into the ink and fill the bogus paper with line patterns. *Note:* Children may put their used cardboard strips on paper towels. Have extra towels available for any spillage. Encourage children to experiment with the way they use the cardboard strips to make ink lines. Use action words like *stamp, blot, drag, twist, brush, zigzag,* and *curve*. (See Illustration 4-4A.) Remove ink from desks.

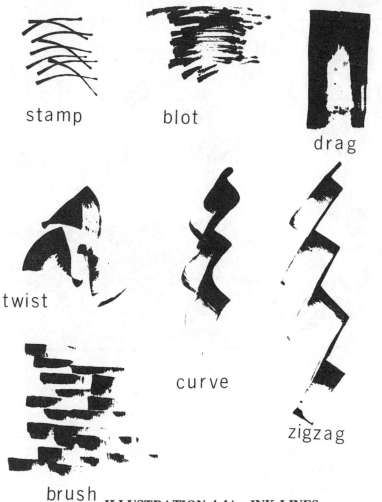

**ILLUSTRATION 4-4A   INK LINES**

- Use the crayons to color in between the dry inked areas. (See Illustration 4-4B.)
  *Note:* Color should be put on in heavy coats. Avoid touching or covering ink lines.
  Gray bogus showing through enhances the composition.

*Can You Imagine . . .*

Cover and bind a child's creative writing collection with "Ink Line" compositions.
Use "Ink Line" compositions for shelf covers.
Create an interesting effect with ink lines on newspaper or patterned wallpaper instead
of bogus paper.

## ETCHINGS IN RECTANGLES (GRADES 5-6)

To etch planned patterns in predesignated areas of scratch board.

**ILLUSTRATION 4-4B**

*You'll Need . . .*

Newspaper • shirt boards or cardboard 8-1/2″ × 11″ or 9″ × 12″ • crayons • facial tissues • etching tools: tongue depressors, plastic forks, ball point pens (need not contain ink) • 3″ × 5″ cards • manila paper 6″ × 9″.

*Procedures . . .*

- Have children find the word *etching* in the dictionary and discuss the meaning.
- Cover desks with newspaper.
- Completely cover shirt boards with heavy coats of bright colors of crayons. *Note:* Encourage children to put on colors so that one color flows into another.
- With the tissue, polish the colors to a high luster.
- Cover the colors completely with a heavy coat of black crayon. *Note:* If, when applying the black crayon, the undercolor appears to peel, apply the black in the opposite direction. That is, if the undercolor is applied vertically, then put on the black horizontally.
- With the tissue, polish the black coat of crayon to a high luster.
- Split the tongue depressor vertically and then break each piece in half horizontally.
- Place the 3″ × 5″ card in one corner on the black coated cardboard and trace around the card with one of the etching tools (pen, fork, or piece of tongue depressor). *Note:*

Children may experiment with all three tools in order to remove the black so that a line of color shows.

- Continue to trace around the card until the entire surface of this scratch board is covered with overlapping rectangles. *Note:* By placing the card so that it overlaps previously drawn shapes, various sized rectangles will be created. (See Illustration 4-5.)

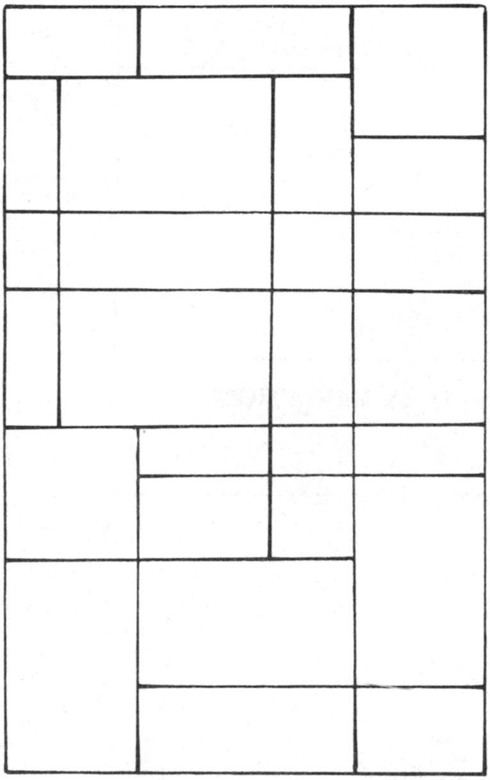

**ILLUSTRATION 4-5**

**SCRATCH BOARD OF RECTANGLES**

- Fold the manila paper into 4 equal parts.
- Fill one section of the manila paper with vertical straight lines, varying the widths of the lines by changing the pressure applied to the crayon or altering the position of the crayon. (See Illustration 4-6A.)
- Fill another section with bent horizontal lines (Illustration 4-6B), and a third section with curved vertical lines (Illustration 4-6C).
- Fill the fourth section with lines that are curved several times and that resemble scalloped lines (Illustration 4-6D).
- Using these line patterns on the manila paper as reference, create different line repetitions in the rectangles on the scratch board by using several of the etching tools. (See Illustration 4-7.) *Note:* The closer together the lines are etched, the stronger the patterns are. About five different sized rectangles may be left completely black.

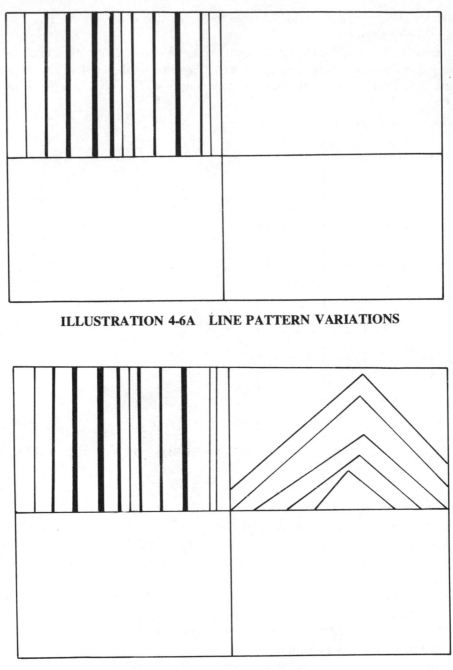

**ILLUSTRATION 4-6A   LINE PATTERN VARIATIONS**

**ILLUSTRATION 4-6B**

*Can You Imagine . . .*

Display "wall to wall" etchings. Append a title on each etching.
Etch scenes from a favorite story on the scratch board.

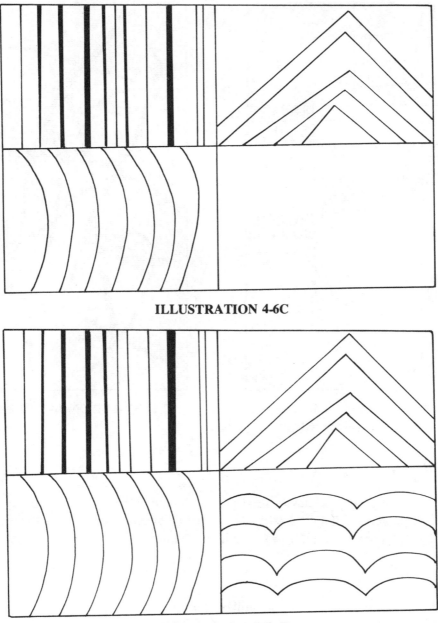

**ILLUSTRATION 4-6C**

**ILLUSTRATION 4-6D**

With the etching tools, trace around leaves. Etch the veins and textures of the surfaces of the leaves.

Collect and display prints of etchings. Discuss line designs in the prints.

## RUB-A-LINE (GRADES K-2)

To make textured rubbings of linear objects.

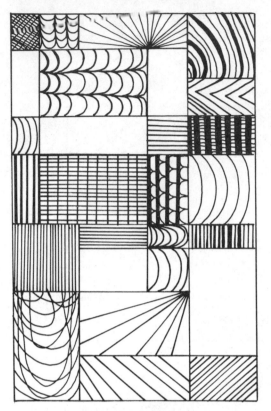

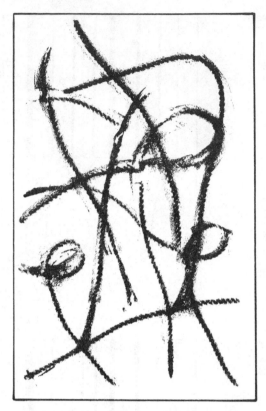

**ILLUSTRATION 4-7**
**ETCHINGS IN RECTANGLES**

**ILLUSTRATION 4-8   RUB-A-LINE**

*You'll Need . . .*

Two or 3 different thicknesses of string 12″ lengths (1 of each thickness per child) •
cardboard strips about 1/2″ × 10″ and 1/4″ × 10″ (1 of each per child) • tracing paper or
manila drawing paper 9″ × 12″ • broken crayons with paper wrapping removed.

*Procedures . . .*

- Have children put a string or cardboard strip on their tables.
- Place the tracing or manila paper on top of the string or cardboard strip.
- Rub crayon on the part of the paper that directly covers the string or cardboard strip
  to pick up a line print of the object. *Note:* The more pressure children apply to the
  crayon, the clearer the rubbing. Paper should be held as still as possible while
  making the rubbing.
- Have children move the string or cardboard strip to different positions under the
  paper and make more rubbings. (See Illustration 4-8.)
- Make other rubbings of different thicknesses of string and of different widths of
  strips, filling the paper with rubbings.

*Can You Imagine . . .*

Place other objects (burlap scrap, drinking straw, toothpick, yarn, ribbon, hairpin, paper clip) under the tracing paper and create a variety of rubbings.

Cut irregular shapes from the rubbings and mount them on a large black background. Leave a small black border around each shape. (See Illustration 4-9.) Hang mounted shapes.

Do rubbings on tracing paper. Tape them on the windows to create a transparent effect.

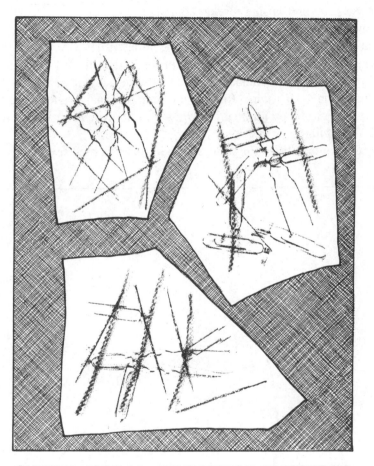

**ILLUSTRATION 4-9   COMPOSITION OF RUBBINGS**

## WIND MOVEMENTS (GRADES 3-4)

To create a "windy" feeling by controlled movement of ink lines on paper.

*You'll Need . . .*

Collection of poems about the wind • newspaper • tongue depressors • twigs • black drawing ink (2 tablespoonsful per child) • jar lids for ink containers • pastel colors of construction paper 12″ × 18″ or manila drawing paper • paper towels.

*Procedures . . .*

- Read several of the poems to the children. Discuss the movement of the wind. Talk about how objects, plants, and people react when disturbed by the wind. Use descriptive phrases like *blowing rain; leaning against the wind; tossed in the wind; pushed, twisted,* and *turned by the wind;* etc.
- Cover the desks with newspaper.
- Have children split the tongue depressors in half vertically.
- Dip twigs and tongue depressor pieces in the black ink and draw lines that suggest wind direction and movement on the construction paper or manila drawing paper. (See Illustration 4-10.) *Note:* Remind children after using a drawing tool to put it on a paper towel until they are ready to draw with it again. Have extra towels available for possible spillage of ink.
- Display the compositions for children to view as you read several of the wind poems again.

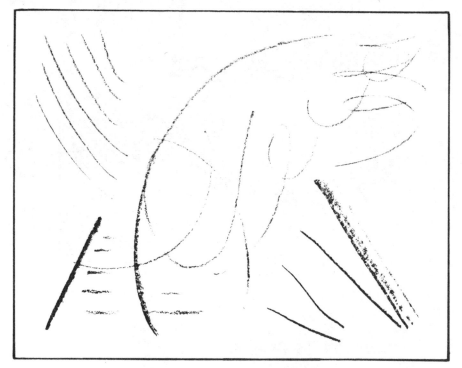

**ILLUSTRATION 4-10  WIND MOVEMENTS**

*Can You Imagine . . .*

Make a three-panel screen by attaching with masking, transparent, or gummed tape three bulletin boards. Mount "Wind Movement" compositions on both sides of the screen. Display the screen for a "walk around" exhibit. As children walk and view the compositions, encourage them to describe what the lines in the different compositions tell them about wind movement.

Attach compositions end to end and then roll them. Play wind music (on piano or record) and have two children slowly unroll the attached composition before the class for a panoramic viewing of the completed project.

Reread some of the wind poems and ask children to select phrases or lines that they think could be used to describe their compositions. Each child writes his or her selection on a strip of lined paper and tapes the printed strip on the composition. Place all compositions together between tagboard covers and tie with yarn to form a book labelled "Wind Movement." Keep the booklet available for independent browsing and reading by children.

## LINES OVER COLOR (GRADES 5-6)

To create a linear composition over prearranged transparent color.

### *You'll Need . . .*

Bottles of different sizes and shapes for a still life drawing • newspaper • assorted colors of tissue paper 4″ × 6″ (3 or 4 colors of each child's choice) • white construction paper 12″ × 18″ • paint brushes • glue and water solution mixed in equal parts (1/4 cup per child) • paint cups for the solution • tongue depressors • twigs • black drawing ink (2 tablespoonsful per child) • jar lids for ink containers • paper towels.

### *Procedures . . .*

- Before the session begins, set up the still life (bottles) on your desk or a table where everyone can see the bottles. Discuss shapes and sizes of bottles in the still life, and have children note that some bottles overlap others. *Note:* Still life should be at about the children's eye level when they are seated.
- Cover the desks with newspaper.
- Have children select three or four colors of tissue paper.
- Tear the tissue paper into different lengths and shapes as suggested in Illustration 4-11A.
- Overlap tissue shapes on the white construction paper as suggested in Illustration 4-11B. *Note:* Children need not cover the entire surface of the construction paper with tissue shapes. White areas may be left to enhance the project.
- With the paint brushes *paint over* the tissue shapes with the glue and water solution so that they adhere to the construction paper. *Note:* Remind children to paint over the edges of all shapes, and to paint out the air bubbles. Let the tissue-coated construction papers dry.
- Split the tongue depressors in half vertically.
- Dip twigs and tongue depressor pieces in black ink and draw a still life of bottle shapes on the tissue-designed construction paper. (See Illustration 4-11C.) *Note:*

**ILLUSTRATION 4-11A   LINES OVER COLOR**

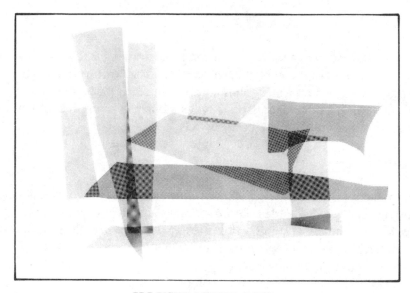

**ILLUSTRATION 4-11B**

Encourage children to draw large. Remind them after using a drawing tool to put it on a paper towel until they are ready to draw with it again. Have extra towels available for possible spillage of ink.

- Turn the still life arrangement about every fifteen minutes so that children see different views to make on the same drawing. (See Illustration 4-11D.) *Note:* Have children overlap bottle shapes. A bottle appearing on the right could appear on the left if the still life were turned to a new position.
- After drawings dry, press them under weight (books, magazines, etc.) to prevent curling.

**ILLUSTRATION 4-11C**

**ILLUSTRATION 4-11D**

*Can You Imagine . . .*

With twigs and tongue depressor pieces and black drawing ink, draw line landscape over tissue shapes.

Do line self-portraits over tissue shapes.

Draw ink lined telephone poles along a highway or lamp posts along a city street on the tissue-designed construction paper.

## LINE ON LINE (GRADES K-2)

To experiment with the line in creating an overlapping arrangement of shapes.

*You'll Need . . .*

Various lengths of rope, string, yarn, and thread • assorted colors of construction paper 4-1/2″ × 6″ (3 colors of each child's choice) • scissors • paste • paste dabbers or brushes.

*Procedures . . .*

- Have children help lay the ropes, string, yarn, and thread on the floor so that the items overlap in vertical and horizontal positions to represent a plaid design. Explain that the rope, string, etc., each represents a line in the design.
- Have children select three colors of construction paper and cut each sheet into strips. *Note:* Strips need not be the same width or length. Explain that strips can be used to show lines.
- Place two strips on the table in any overlapping position. *Note:* Remind children that they have shown two lines using two of their strips. Reproduce on the board several examples of the line arrangements children created.
- Have children secure the arrangement by applying paste where the two strips overlap.
- Create a large shape from the two-strip arrangement by pasting on more strips in overlapping positions, leaving space between at least two strips that another strip overlaps. (See Illustration 4-12.) *Note:* Encourage children to use all three colors in their creations. Discuss ways to expand a shape (rather than stack the strips), for example: putting some strips end to end, and crossing two or more strips spaced apart with other strips spaced apart.

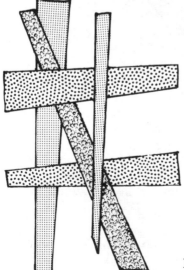

**ILLUSTRATION 4-12   LINE ON LINE**

*Can You Imagine* . . .

Create three- and four-sided shapes by stapling various arrangements together. Suspend them with string to create see-through mobiles.

Create a "crosshatch" wall. Mount "Line on Line" shapes in overlapping positions on a wall.

Have a "Look, Think, Tell" session. Paste shape creations on white background. Display one mounted creation at a time for children to study and tell as many different things as it looks like.

## WEAVING COLORS (GRADES 3-4)

To understand the basic steps involved in simple paper weaving.

*You'll Need* . . .

Collection of woven objects: basket, pot holder, knitted sweater, table placemat, or similar items • 3 packages of assorted colors of construction paper 9" × 12" • scissors • paste • paste dabbers or brushes.

*Procedures* . . .

- Have children read a dictionary meaning of *weave*. Show them the woven objects. Call attention to the over and under arrangement of the threads in the weave.
- Print the following color groups (see Chapter 2) in a list on the chalkboard: 2 warm and 1 cool, 2 cool and 1 warm, 2 bright and 1 dull, 2 dull and 1 bright.
- Have children each select three sheets of construction paper of colors specified by the color group they choose from the list on the board.
- Cut the three sheets of paper in half.
- Cut one of the pieces of each color in half so there are three pieces of each color selected. (See Illustration 4-13.)

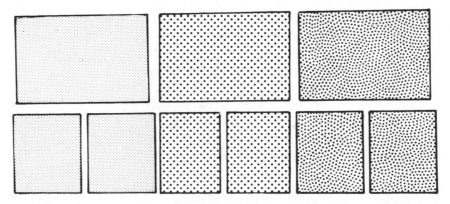

**ILLUSTRATION 4-13  DIVIDING PAPER INTO THREE PARTS**

- Stack the pieces of paper in three groups so that there are three colors in each group and the three pieces of paper in the individual groups are the same size.
- In each group, fold any one of the pieces of paper in half. (See Illustration 4-14A.)
- Make a 1/2″ fold along the ends opposite the fold. (See Illustration 4-14B.)
- Unfold the two ends as shown in Illustration 4-14C.
- Cut up from the fold a series of slits, stopping about 1/2″ from the opposite side where the ends had been folded. (See Illustration 4-14D.) *Note:* Children do not have to leave the same width between slits. When the paper is opened, there should be a series of long slits surrounded by a border. (See Illustration 4-14E.)

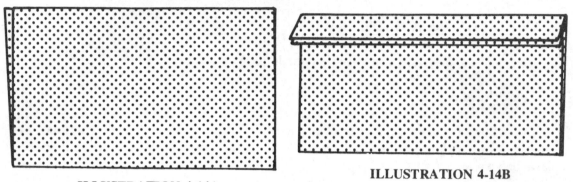

**ILLUSTRATION 4-14A**

**ILLUSTRATION 4-14B**

**EXECUTING A SIMPLE WEAVE**

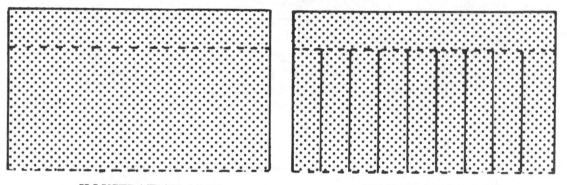

**ILLUSTRATION 4-14C**

**ILLUSTRATION 4-14D**

- In each group, cut the remaining two pieces of paper into strips to represent lines. *Note:* Before children cut the paper into strips, have them put the two sheets of paper from a group beside the slitted paper from that same group so they will know which way the two pieces will need to be cut into strips that are long enough for weaving.
- Weave these strips one at a time over and under the slits of the first piece of paper from the group. (See Illustration 4-14F.) *Note:* The important thing to remember in paper weaving is if the first strip woven is started over the end of the slitted paper, then the second strip is inserted under the end of the slitted paper. Or, the reverse of this procedure may be followed. This process is repeated until there is no more space for additional strips. (See Illustration 4-14G.) Encourage the use of various color

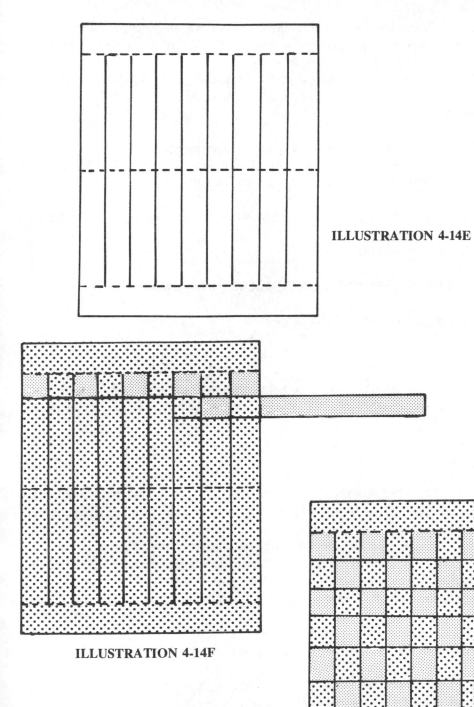

**ILLUSTRATION 4-14E**

**ILLUSTRATION 4-14F**

**ILLUSTRATION 4-14G**

combinations. For example, if a child selects red, yellow, and blue, he can make any three of the following: a red and yellow weave; a red and blue weave; a blue and yellow weave; a red, yellow, and blue weave.

- Secure the woven strips by putting a small amount of paste under ends of strips.

*Can You Imagine . . .*

Make smaller sample weaves from scraps and paste on notebook covers.

Weave colored construction paper strips on small, slitted paper rectangles. Add patches of paper to represent doors and windows. Arrange on long brown kraft paper to create a paper woven city scene.

Make a textured cube by covering all sides of a box with overlapping individual paper weaves.

Make a panel of paper woven designs.

## THREE WEAVES OF DIFFERENT CONFIGURATIONS (GRADES 5-6)

To create paper woven designs of irregular shapes.

*You'll Need . . .*

Collection of woven objects: basket, potholder, knitted sweater, table placemat, or similar items • 3 packages of assorted colors of construction paper 9" × 12" • scissors • paste • paste dabbers or brushes.

*Procedures . . .*

- Discuss the meaning of *weaving*. Display the collected woven objects for children to examine the over and under arrangements of the threads creating the patterned surfaces.
- Have children each select one light and one dark color of construction paper.
- From one sheet, free cut three large, different geometric shapes (square, circle, diamond, triangle, etc.) so that as much of the paper as possible is used.
- Place each of these shapes on the other piece of construction paper and trace around them.
- Cut out the traced shapes.
- Make three groups of the shapes by putting shapes of the same configuration together.
- Fold one of the shapes from each group in half.
- Cut up from the fold a series of slits, stopping about 1/2" from the opposite open ends. (See Illustration 4-15.)

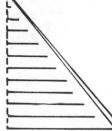

**ILLUSTRATION 4-15   WEAVE FORM**

● Cut the remaining shapes into strips to represent different kinds of lines: wavy, zigzagged, curved, straight, etc. (See Illustration 4-16.)

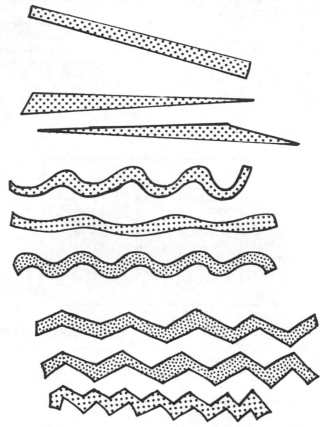

**ILLUSTRATION 4-16   PAPER STRIPS OF DIFFERENT CONFIGURATIONS**

● Weave these strips one at a time over and under the slits of each of the folded, slitted shapes. Create an interesting weave by combining different strips or using an unusual shaped strip in repetition. (See Illustration 4-17.) *Note:* The important thing to remember in paper weaving is if the first strip woven is started under the end of the slitted paper, then the second strip is inserted over the end of the slitted paper. Or, the reverse of this procedure may be followed. This process is repeated until there is no more space for additional strips.
● Cut off portions of strips that extend over the outer edges of the slitted shape.
● Put a small amount of paste under ends of the strips to secure them.

*Can You Imagine . . .*

Add construction paper head, neck, arms, legs, and feet to the weaves to create "weavy people."

Cover boxes of different sizes and shapes with paper weaves spotted with paste-on

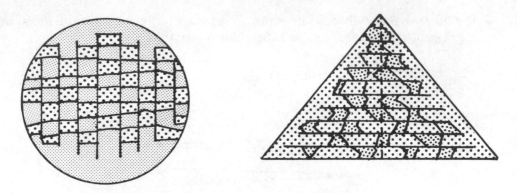

**ILLUSTRATION 4-17   THREE WEAVES OF DIFFERENT CONFIGURATIONS**

doors and windows. Set covered boxes on a surface of paper woven sidewalks surrounded by paper woven fences.

Make a still life of paper woven leaf, fruit, or vase shapes.

# CHAPTER 5

# PATTERN IN REPETITION

Pattern, like color, is everywhere. Pattern may be the result of repetition in color, shape, line, size, spacing, or texture arrangement. More than one of these attributes may be involved to achieve the creation of various simple and complicated patterns. An arrangement of trees, for example, may create a pattern because of repetition in size; repetition in size and color; or repetition in size, shape, and spacing.

This chapter introduces children to a new perspective of the true meaning of pattern as they observe pattern created by nature and man, and as they experiment with line, shape, color, size, spacing, and texture in repetition.

## BEFORE YOU BEGIN

Show objects or cloth that have patterns. Help children arrive at a definition for *pattern* as they view and describe the items. Help them understand that patterns are formed the instant an arrangement of two or more things, persons, or places is assembled. Remind the class that lines can form patterns, that lines can form shapes which form patterns, and that man creates patterns and nature creates patterns. Explain that a pattern can be regular or irregular. A regular pattern remains exactly the same no matter how often shape, color, spacing, size, and arrangement are repeated. (See Figure 5-1.)

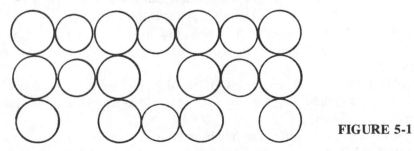

**FIGURE 5-1**

Ask children to point out examples of regular patterns in weaves in their clothing and in objects around the room. Lines and spaces on the chalkboard, the floor design, windows and desks are examples of regular pattern repetition.

An irregular pattern can have at least one attribute that remains the same while at least one other attribute varies. The same shape, for example, can be repeated but its size could vary. (See Figure 5-2.) The same shape and size could be repeated and the spacing can vary. (See Figure 5-3.) Likewise, the same shape, size, and spacing can be repeated and the color could vary.

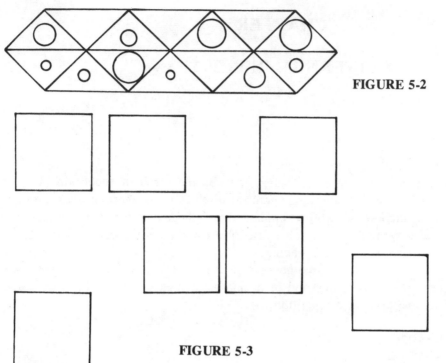

**FIGURE 5-2**

**FIGURE 5-3**

Have children experiment with arranging their tables or desks in the room so that an irregular pattern is formed from variation in spacing between desks.

Play "Hunt the Pattern." Each child folds a 9″ × 12″ sheet of manila paper into eight equal parts and draws samples of regular patterns he sees around him. To help the class begin, suggest that they observed patterns formed by desks, by crayons in a box, by lines on the chalkboard, and by a stack of objects like books, and make simple drawings of these. (See Figure 5-4.) Encourage children to locate other patterns to draw.

On the reverse side of the paper, children find and draw irregular patterns (Figure 5-5), for example: a row of library books, children in a line, weaves in someone's clothing, chairs in a row, leaves on a plant.

Encourage children to bring in examples of regular and irregular patterns from magazines, newspaper, photographs and from the natural world in which they live. Display and discuss the pattern repetitions.

An excellent use of man-made pattern can be observed in the surface designs of African sculpture. (See Figure 5-6.) Plan a trip to the art museum and visit the African art galleries. Children in grades four through six may take sketch pads and do quick, simple sketches of patterns found on the sculptures.

FIGURE 5-4          FIGURE 5-5

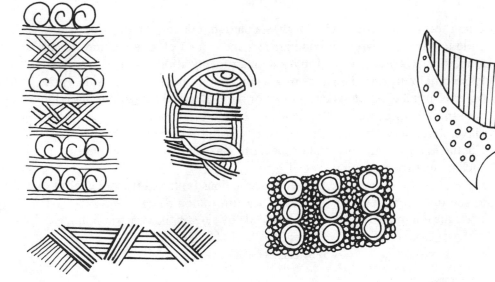

FIGURE 5-6

Obtain prints and reproductions of African sculpture from art museum shops and libraries. Bring in some of the following books (or substitute ones of similar content): *The Art of Africa*,[1] *African Sculpture*,[2] *African Mythology*,[3] *African Sculpture*,[4] *Contemporary Art in Africa*.[5] Place the reproductions and books on a table where children may examine them in their spare time. Put pencils and paper on the table, too, so that children may sketch examples of pattern repetition. Save the sketches for reference for the following projects of this chapter: "Round Masks Grouping," "Masks Inseparable," and "Mask Reflections." The art prints and references will be needed also for these projects.

## DRESS A PAIR (GRADES K-2)

To use the basic characteristics of pattern repetition in composition.

*You'll Need . . .*

Brown kraft paper 12″ × 10″ (2 sheets per child) • scissors • a story version of "The Gingerbread Boy" • assorted colors of felt scraps about 2″ × 2″ (3 or 4 per child) • assorted colors of yarn 3″ lengths (3 or 4 per child) • paste • paste dabbers or brushes • assorted colors of construction paper 10″ × 10″ (1 color of each child's choice).

*Procedures . . .*

- Read or tell the story of "The Gingerbread Boy." Discuss the shape of the cookie in the story. Ask children if they have ever seen a cookie decorated with icing. What decorations were made? What colors were used?
- Fold a sheet of kraft paper in half lengthwise.
- Starting on the fold, free cut a half gingerbread boy shape as suggested in Illustration 5-1.
- Using this cutout (Illustration 5-2) as a pattern, cut enough of these shapes for each child to have two. *Note:* Second graders and some first graders may be able to cut a gingerbread boy pattern and make another identical one from it.
- Have children place their two paper gingerbread boys side by side on their desk. *Note:* Remind children whenever two or more identical shapes are placed together, a pattern is formed.
- Have children select three or four scraps of felt and three or four lengths of yarn.
- Cut the felt and yarn into smaller shapes to make the *same* decorations (hair, buttons, socks, etc.) for *both* gingerbread boys.
- Have children arrange and paste the decorations on the gingerbread boys and check to see that both look exactly alike. (See Illustration 5-3.)
- Paste the completed gingerbread boys side by side on the construction paper squares.

[1]Elsy Leuzinger, *The Art of Africa*. New York: Crown Publishers, 1960.
[2]Ladislas Segy, *African Sculpture*. New York: Dover Public, 1958.
[3]Geoffrey Parrinder, *African Mythology*. London: Paul Hamlyn, 1967.
[4]William Fagg and Margaret Plass, *African Sculpture*. New York: E. P. Dutton, Vista, 1964.
[5]Ulli Beier, *Contemporary Art in Africa*. New York: Frederick A. Praeger, 1968.

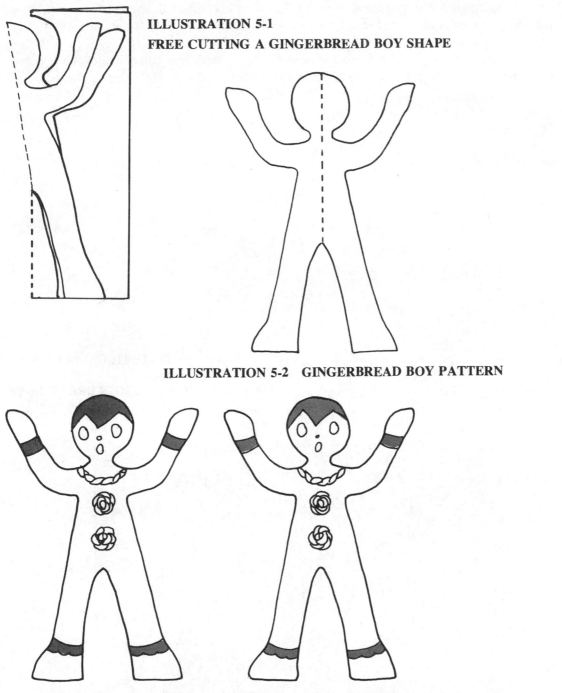

**ILLUSTRATION 5-1
FREE CUTTING A GINGERBREAD BOY SHAPE**

**ILLUSTRATION 5-2   GINGERBREAD BOY PATTERN**

**ILLUSTRATION 5-3   A PAIR OF DRESSED GINGERBREAD BOYS**

*Can You Imagine . . .*

Paste each pair of decorated gingerbread boys back to back. Punch a small hole in the head. Put a string through the hole and suspend from overhead.

Paste decorated gingerbread boys on lightweight cardboard and cut them out. With masking tape or paste, attach cardboard supports (Illustration 5-4) to the backs and stand them in pairs on library shelves and tables.

Around the completed gingerbread boys on the construction paper squares, paste pieces of string to create line designs. (See Illustration 5-5.)

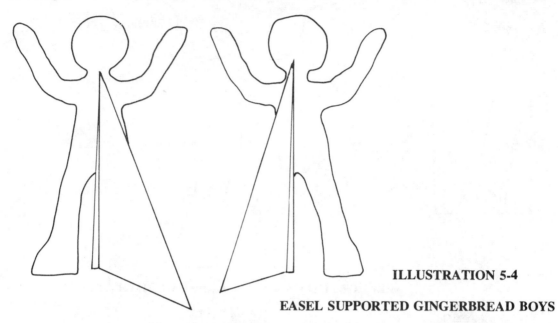

**ILLUSTRATION 5-4**

**EASEL SUPPORTED GINGERBREAD BOYS**

**ILLUSTRATION 5-5   GINGERBREAD BOYS WITH LINEAR DESIGN**

**WHAT'S IN A LEAF? (GRADES 3-4)**

To use a natural pattern in a composition.

*You'll Need* . . .

Manila paper 9″ × 12″ • pencils • leaves that have been pressed individually between two pieces of waxed paper under a book or weight for at least a week prior to the lesson • white construction paper 12″ × 12″ (2 per child) • white crayons • black cakes of water color • paper towels • paint cups for water • water (about 1/4 cup per child) • #12 paintbrushes • black construction paper 18″ × 24″ • paste • paste dabbers or brushes.

*Procedures* . . .

- Take the class for a walk to observe the natural patterns formed by nature. Call attention to shape repetition of leaves on a plant, petal repetition on flowers, etc.
- On the manila paper with pencil, have children draw the vein pattern (Illustration 5-6A) of a pressed leaf without drawing the leaf outline. *Note:* To illustrate, you may want to make a sample drawing of a vein pattern on the chalkboard. Encourage children to vary the line thickness and include a leaf stem if there is one.

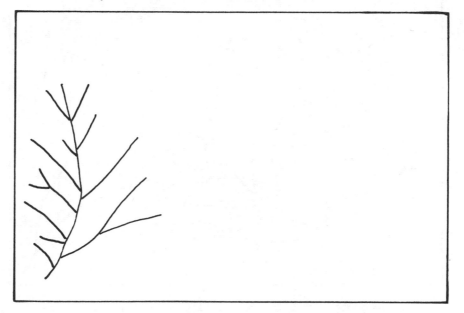

**ILLUSTRATION 5-6A   VEIN PATTERN**

- Turn the leaf to a different position and draw another vein pattern as suggested in Illustration 5-6B. *Note:* Ask children to look for more veins to include as they repeat the drawing.
- On one white construction paper square, using the white crayon, draw several vein

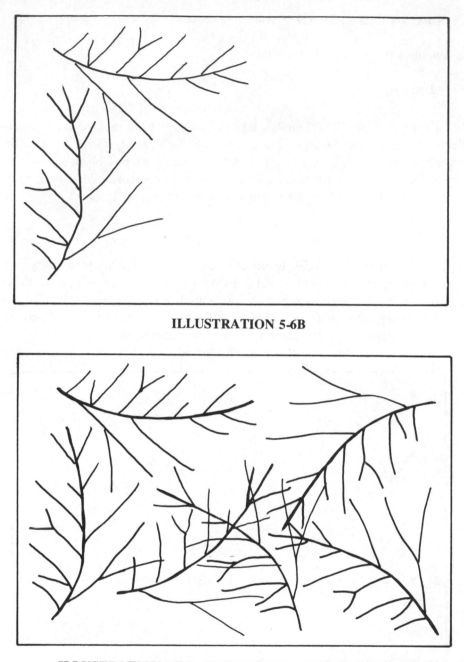

**ILLUSTRATION 5-6B**

**ILLUSTRATION 5-7A   REPETITION OF VEIN PATTERN**

patterns of the leaf in different positions. (See Illustration 5-7A.) *Note:* Encourage children to use the pencilled drawings as reference. The white crayon on white construction paper will be dimly visible only closeup. These drawings may or may not overlap. Stress the importance of varying the thickness of the line.

• Place the cake of water color on a paper towel and moisten with water.

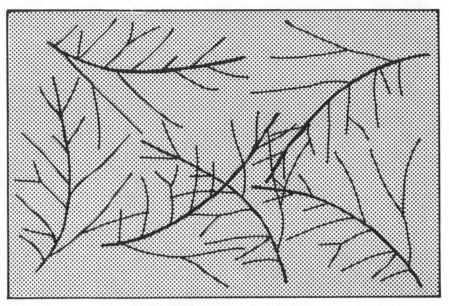

**ILLUSTRATION 5-7B**

- Brush the water color lightly over the vein pattern drawings on the white construction paper. (See Illustration 5-7B.) *Note:* Place this brush painting aside to dry.
- On the other white construction paper square, using the white crayon, trace around the leaf.
- Continue to trace the leaf, turning it in a new direction for each tracing and allowing the leaf to touch a previous tracing at some point. (See Illustration 5-8A.)

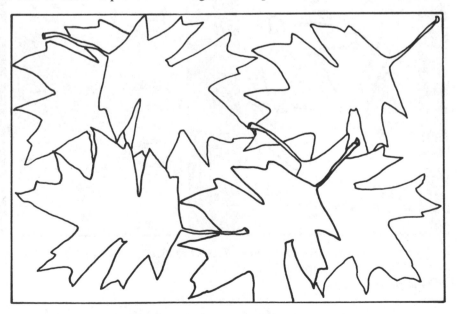

**ILLUSTRATION 5-8A   LEAF REPETITION**

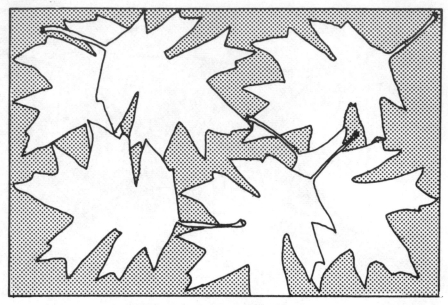

**ILLUSTRATION 5-8B**

- Moisten again the cake of water color with water.
- Paint the space between leaf shapes (Illustration 5-8B) *or* paint the leaves. *Note:* Remind the children *not* to paint both.
- With paste mount both leaf compositions side by side on the black construction paper. (See Illustration 5-9.)

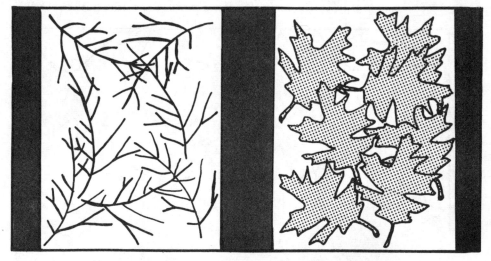

**ILLUSTRATION 5-9   PAINTED LEAF PATTERN**

*Can You Imagine . . .*

Use green water color to paint the leaf compositions for a Spring project.

Make "What's in Tree Bark?" composition. On 12″ white construction paper square, using white crayon, reproduce the pattern in a piece of tree bark. Fill the paper with this pattern. Brush gray, violet, or brown water color lightly over the pattern drawing. Glue the piece of bark or a part of it in a corner of the paper. Mount the composition and display.

On a 12″ white construction paper square, using white crayon, trace around the leaf. Fill the paper with traced leaf shapes. With green, orange, red, or yellow water color, paint the leaf shapes. Cut around the outline of the total composition as suggested in Illustration 5-10. Use this cutout shape for a placemat.

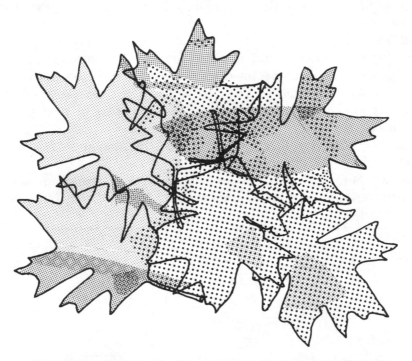

**ILLUSTRATION 5-10   PLACEMAT OF LEAF PATTERNS**

## COLOR ME PATTERN (GRADES 5-6)

To create the illusion of shapes by using a rhythmical linear pattern in varied directions.

*You'll Need . . .*

Fashion and sports magazines (1 of each per child) • scissors • manila paper 9″ × 12″ • pencils • assorted colors of construction paper (except black) 18″ × 24″ (1 color of each child's choice) • different colors (except yellow) or all black felt markers (1 per child).

*Procedures . . .*

• Children browse through the magazines and cut out three or four full-length fashion models or sports figures. *Note:* The most interesting effects of this project are achieved by using models and sports figures in action poses.

- On the manila paper, children draw a small circle shape about 2″ in diameter, *very lightly* with a pencil. (See Illustration 5-11A.) *Note:* The drawing should be so light that it can only be seen close-up.
- Add a very lightly drawn rectangular shape that appears partially hidden by the circle as suggested in Illustration 5-11B. *Note:* On the chalkboard you may want to draw along with the class to illustrate this procedure.
- Fill the circle with pencilled parallel lines that are as close together as possible. (See Illustration 5-11C.)
- Fill the rectangular shape with pencilled parallel lines that are as close together as possible and that run in a different direction from those in the circle. (See Illustration 5-11D.) *Note:* Explain that the patterns created within the two shapes are linear. If outlines of the circle and rectangle are very light and the lines carefully drawn close together within the outlines, the linear patterns create an illusion of a circle and a rectangle.
- Add two other very lightly drawn shapes (Illustration 5-11E) to the circle and rectangle.
- Fill each of these shapes with pencilled, vertical, horizontal, or slanted lines.
- On the construction paper, trace around one of the magazine figures *very lightly* with

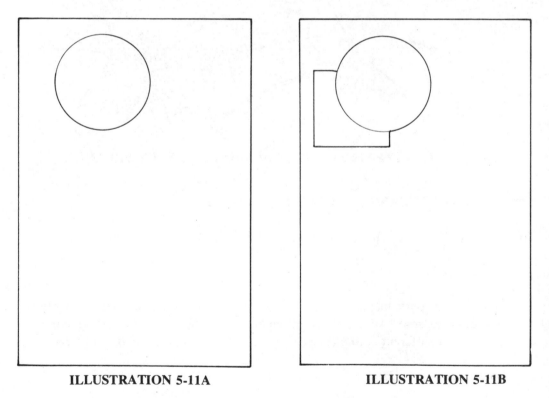

**ILLUSTRATION 5-11A**          **ILLUSTRATION 5-11B**

**FORMING SHAPES WITH LINEAR DESIGNS**

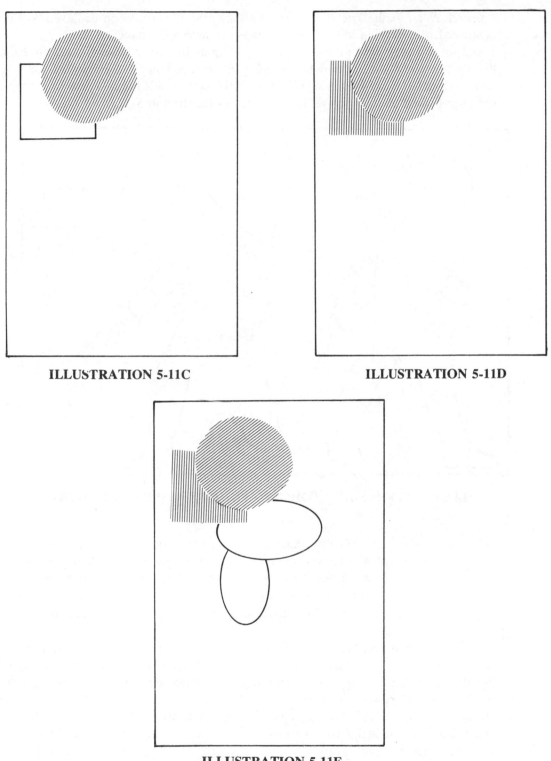

**ILLUSTRATION 5-11C**

**ILLUSTRATION 5-11D**

**ILLUSTRATION 5-11E**

a pencil. *Note:* If the line is the least bit dark, the illusion to be achieved will be destroyed. Refer children to their drawings on the manila paper.

- Make several very light tracings of the same figure and/or of other figures cut from the magazines. *Note:* Traced figures may be grouped in twos or threes, or may appear singularly. All figures need not be on the same level. Figures may touch or be partially behind another figure as suggested in Illustration 5-12A.

**ILLUSTRATION 5-12A   FORMING FIGURES AND BACKGROUND**

- Select a color of construction paper and a marker. *Note:* If various colored felt markers (instead of all black) are available, encourage children to consider an unusual color combination, for example: two different values of a color—red marker and pink paper; a warm color and cool color—red marker and pale blue paper. If only black markers are available, discourage the selection of a very dark color of paper.
- With the felt marker, fill in a silhouette figure with linear design, using either vertical, horizontal, or slanted lines drawn as closely together as possible. (See Illustration 5-12B.) *Note:* Figures are not to be outlined with the marker. Refer children to their pencilled drawings.
- Fill in other figures with linear designs. *Note:* When one figure overlaps another, in order that each maintains its own identity, change the linear direction (Illustration 5-12C) within the figure.

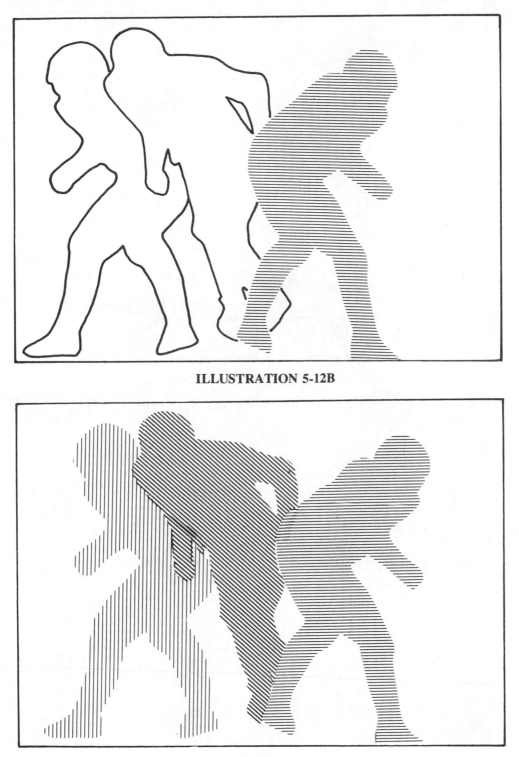

**ILLUSTRATION 5-12B**

**ILLUSTRATION 5-12C**

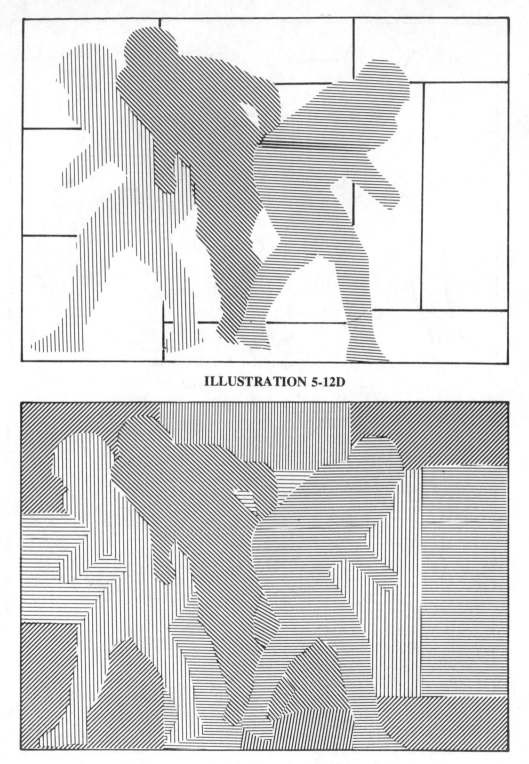

**ILLUSTRATION 5-12D**

**ILLUSTRATION 5-12E**

- Draw light pencilled geometric shapes that overlap to break up the background behind the figures. (See Illustration 5-12D.)
- Add *light* pencilled vertical and/or horizontal linear pattern to fill in these shapes as was done on manila practice paper. (See Illustration 5-12E.) *Note:* Explain that the background linear pattern should be placed so that no portion of a figure becomes a part of the background, that is, vertical or horizontal lines of a figure should not become fused with vertical and horizontal lines behind the figure.

### *Can You Imagine . . .*

Combine other patterns with linear patterns to create a different effect.

Use two colored markers instead of one to make the linear patterns.

Cut the completed compositions into diamond, triangular, and rectangular shapes. Place edges of shapes together and cover a wall with linear compositions of geometric shapes.

## PATTERNS 'ROUND A CYLINDER (GRADES K-2)

To combine a group of patterned strips and create a composition of regular and irregular patterns.

### *You'll Need . . .*

Colored construction paper strips 3″ × 18″ (1 strip of each child's choice) • colored construction paper 6″ × 4-1/2″ (2 colors of each child's choice) • scissors • paste • paste dabbers or brushes • 4 to 7 sheets of black construction paper 18″ × 24″ • newspaper to cover a table • waxed paper to cover newspaper • shellac • paintbrushes • 1/2 jar of turpentine.

### *Procedures . . .*

- Draw a square, circle, and triangle on the chalkboard. Review names of these shapes with the children. Explain that these basic shapes may vary. Draw a variation of each as suggested in Illustration 5-13.
- Have children each select one color strip 3″ × 18″, and two different colors of the 6″ × 4-1/2″ construction paper. *Note:* If children have carried out the projects in Chapter 2, have them select one warm color and two cool colors of paper, or one cool color and two warm colors.
- From the two pieces of 6″ × 4-1/2″ paper, have children free cut circle, square, and triangle shapes that are small enough to be pasted on the 3″ × 18″ strip.
- Paste the cutout shapes on the 3″ × 18″ strip to create a pattern of shapes. *Note:* Encourage children to paste smaller shapes on some of the larger shapes in order to make more interesting patterns. Make a few examples to show the class (Illustration 5-14), but encourage them to think of different pattern arrangements. It is not necessary to use all shapes.
- Cover about 3 inches of one 18″ edge of each sheet of the 18″ × 24″ black construc-

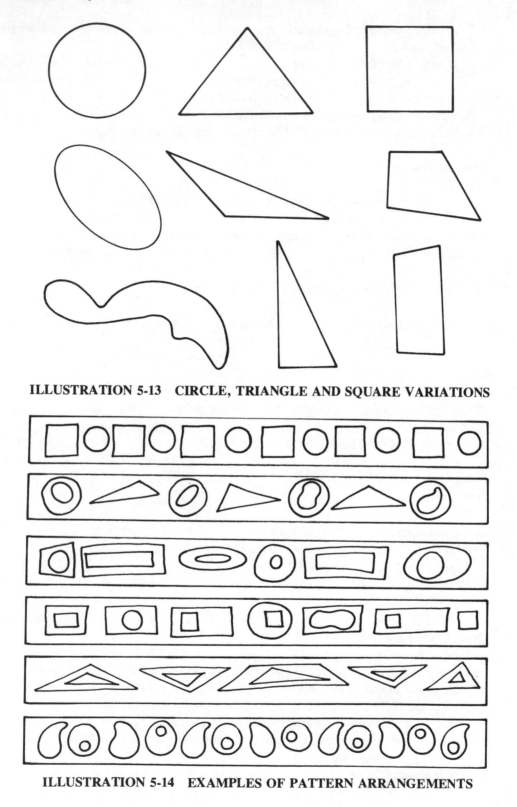

**ILLUSTRATION 5-13    CIRCLE, TRIANGLE AND SQUARE VARIATIONS**

**ILLUSTRATION 5-14    EXAMPLES OF PATTERN ARRANGEMENTS**

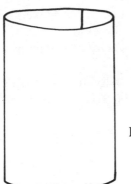

**ILLUSTRATION 5-15A**

tion paper with paste and overlap this edge with the opposite end to form a cylinder. (See Illustration 5-15A.)

- On a cylinder paste one of the children's patterned strips as suggested in Illustration 5-15B.
- Paste on other strips until the cylinder is completely covered. (See Illustration 5-15C.)

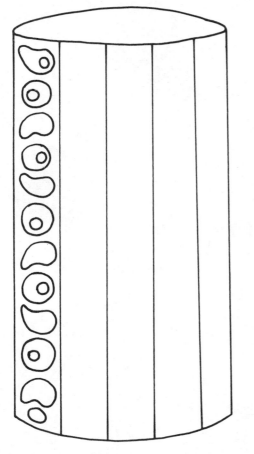

**ILLUSTRATION 5-15B**

**ILLUSTRATION 5-15C**
**PATTERNS 'ROUND A CYLINDER**

- Cover the other cylinders with children's patterned strips. *Note:* Make more cylinders if necessary in order to mount all strips made by the children.
- Cover a table with a layer of newspaper and then with a layer of waxed paper. Place the shellac and brushes on the table.
- Paint over the cylinders of patterns with shellac. *Note:* Individual or small groups of children may take turns helping you shellac the cylinders. To clean the brushes, soak them in turpentine. Place cylinders on waxed paper to dry.

*Can You Imagine . . . .*

Group the cylinders in twos and threes on a low table for a "walk around" display.

Stand the cylinders side by side in a row on a table, bench, or chairs to form dividers for work areas or for displaying children's work papers.

Punch a small hole about 3″ from each end of each strip. Stack about six strips together and put a round head through the holes at each end. Fasten the round heads. Spread the strips to form a round shape. Attach a string to the end of the round head and hang as a mobile. (See Illustration 5-16.) Make mobiles of the other patterned strips.

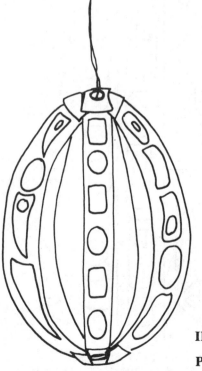

**ILLUSTRATION 5-16**

**PATTERNED SPHERICAL MOBILE**

## SCENES IN PATTERNED SETTINGS (GRADES 3-4)

To create patterned silhouettes and group them in a composition on a patterned background.

*You'll Need . . .*

A swatch of gingham and of pattered calico (optional) • the poem "The Gingham Dog and the Calico Cat" by Eugene Fields • collection of dog and cat pictures • stuffed toy dog and cat (optional) • brown kraft paper 10″ × 24″ • scissors • gray bogus paper 10″ × 15″ • crayons • patterned cloth scraps, burlap and felt scraps about 6″ × 9″ (3 scraps per child) • paste • paste dabbers or brushes • printed wallpaper samples.

*Procedures . . .*

- Show the gingham and calico swatches. Have children read dictionary meanings of *gingham* and *calico*. Help them observe that both pieces of cloth contain patterns.
- Read "The Gingham Dog and the Calico Cat" to the class. Ask children to name objects mentioned in the poem, such as dog, cat, table, clock, chimney, etc. Ask them to name other objects that might have been in the room where the dog and cat were, for example: chair, window, lamp, etc.
- Show the pictures of dogs and cats and compare them with the stuffed toy animals.
- From the brown kraft paper, have children free cut a dog shape, a cat shape (Illustration 5-17) and other objects (Illustration 5-18) mentioned in the poem. *Note:* Explain that shapes will be assembled on the bogus paper so that children will consider spacing with which they will work as they cut these shapes. Show a piece of bogus paper.
- Free cut other objects that might have been in the room where the gingham dog and calico cat were. *Note:* Have more kraft paper available for children who might need or request it.
- Draw around the paper cat or dog pattern on a cloth scrap. *Note:* Have children place the pattern close to one edge of the cloth so that there will be room to place other patterns.

**ILLUSTRATION 5-17   DOG AND CAT SHAPES**

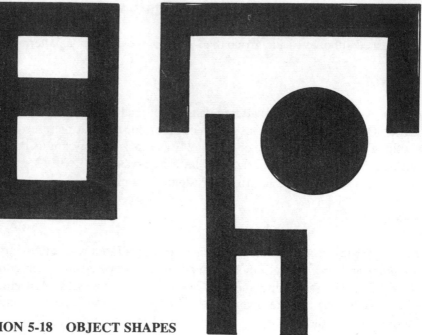

**ILLUSTRATION 5-18   OBJECT SHAPES**

- Place other patterns on the cloth and trace around them. *Note:* Use other cloth scraps as needed.
- Cut out each traced shape.
- Create a scene from the poem by arranging and pasting the cloth scraps on the bogus paper. *Note:* Read the poem to the class again. Remind them that the animals are not always sitting side by side on the table. This should encourage some children to create "the fight" scene, or an "after the fight" scene. (See Illustration 5-19A.)
- Show the wallpaper samples and have children create a patterned wallpaper background with crayon on the bogus paper as suggested in Illustration 5-19B.
- Make crayoned patterns on the floor of the scene to complete the composition. (See Illustration 5-19C.)

*Can You Imagine . . .*

Shellac the completed compositions three times, allowing them to dry after each application. Mount compositions on 18″ × 24″ white construction paper.

Use another poem of each child's preference to create a collection of poems with patterned cloth illustrations for the library.

Show the wallpaper samples. With crayon, children cover the bogus paper with a wallpaper pattern of their own creation. With black crayon draw a scene from the poem on the patterned bogus paper, using only outline shapes. From the cloth scraps, cut details and decorations (clock hands, cat ears, dog whiskers, chair rounds, etc.) to paste on items in the scene.

**ILLUSTRATION 5-19A   SCENES IN PATTERNED SETTINGS**

**ILLUSTRATION 5-19B**

**ILLUSTRATION 5-19C**

## LINEAR PATTERN ANALYSIS (GRADES 5-6)

To isolate a pattern and use it in a composition involving repetition.

*You'll Need . . .*

Index cards 3″ × 5″ (2 per child) • scissors • magazines (preferably fashion and home decorating) • pencils • paste • paste dabbers or brushes • white drawing paper 12″ × 18″ • crayons • tissues.

*Procedures . . .*

- Fold one index card in half.
- Starting on the fold, cut out a rectangular shape so that when the card is opened a ''window'' will be formed. (See Illustration 5-20.)

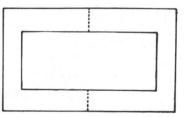

**ILLUSTRATION 5-20   WINDOW VIEWER**

● Place the "window" on a page of a magazine and move the "window" slowly over the page and look for a pattern through the "window" (Illustration 5-21). *Note:* Children may need to examine more than one page in this manner in order to find a pattern.

**ILLUSTRATION 5-21   ISOLATED PATTERN FROM A COMPOSITION**

● Draw around the pattern along the inner edge of the "window" with the pencil.
● Cut out the area of the pattern outlined and place it aside.
● Find, outline, and cut out at least four more magazine patterns. (See Illustration 5-22.)
● Select and paste the most interesting pattern on the whole index card as suggested in Illustration 5-23A. *Note:* Encourage children to consider shapes and colors involved in the pattern in making their selections.
● On the edges of the index card number from 1 to 4 (in any order) the four sides of the pattern. (See Illustration 5-23B.)
● Fold the drawing paper in half lengthwise and in half widthwise.
● Beside the unfolded drawing paper, place the pattern so that the numeral 1 is at the bottom of the card.
● In the *left space at the top* of the drawing paper, draw the pattern with a pencil as viewed in the no. 1 position. (See Illustration 5-24A.) *Note:* The pattern should fill the entire space.

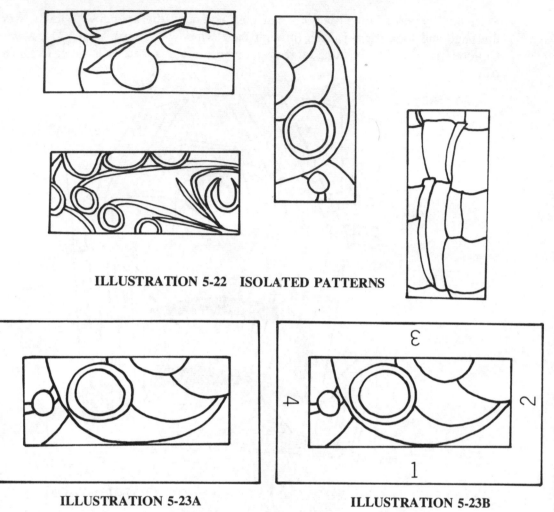

**ILLUSTRATION 5-22   ISOLATED PATTERNS**

**ILLUSTRATION 5-23A**                    **ILLUSTRATION 5-23B**

**NUMBERED POSITIONS FOR PATTERN**

- Turn the card to the second position so that the numeral 2 is at the bottom.
- Copy the pattern in the *top space on the right*. (See Illustration 5-24B.) *Note:* Notice that shapes in the second drawing appear in different positions from the same shapes in the first drawing because the pattern was viewed from a different position. Lines of the pattern are to be extended to fill the entire space.
- In the *bottom space on the left* of the drawing paper, draw the pattern in position no. 3. (See Illustration 5-24C.)
- In the *last space* draw the pattern in position no. 4 (Illustration 5-24D).
- Make the four separate drawings into a single drawing by extending selected pattern lines across each fold into the next space. (See Illustration 5-24E.) *Note:* Perfection of patterns is not important.

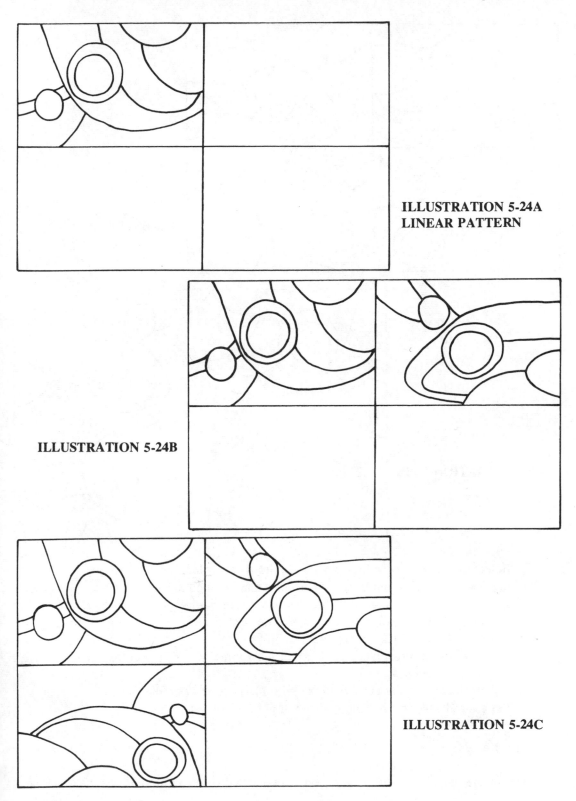

**ILLUSTRATION 5-24A
LINEAR PATTERN**

**ILLUSTRATION 5-24B**

**ILLUSTRATION 5-24C**

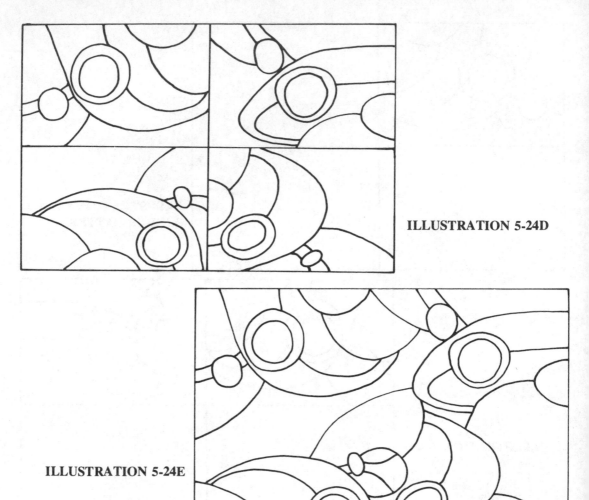

ILLUSTRATION 5-24D

ILLUSTRATION 5-24E

- Select five colors of crayon. *Note:* Write these color descriptions in a list on the chalkboard for children to choose from in making their selections: five warm colors, five cool colors, some warm colors and some cool colors (total five), five dull colors, five bright colors, five values of one color. Review meanings of the descriptions if necessary. (See Chapters 2 and 3.)
- Color all areas of each section with at least three of the five colors. *Note:* Crayon should be applied heavily.
- Polish the completed compositions with the tissue to obtain a sheen.
- Go over all the original lines of the drawing with black crayon.

## Can You Imagine . . .

Mount the completed composition on plywood with white glue and use as a plaque.

Use only one color of different values on the composition. (See Chapter 3.)

Paste the selected magazine pattern within the completed composition.

## ROUND MASKS GROUPING (GRADES K-2)

To reproduce and use patterns discovered in designs.

*You'll Need . . .*

Five or more prints of African masks at least 5″ × 7″ • manila paper 9″ × 12″ • scissors • construction paper of browns, beiges, grays 9″ × 12″ (1 color of each child's choice) • crayons (1 color of each child's choice) • red, yellow, and blue felt scraps about 2″ × 3″ (3 pieces of each child's choice) • paste • paste dabbers or brushes • children's patterns from "Before You Begin" activity • 5 sheets of black construction paper 18″ × 24″ or 5′ length of brown kraft paper (from roll of kraft paper) • masking tape.

*Procedures . . .*

- Show reproductions of African masks for children to observe differences in shapes (Illustration 5-25), facial features (Illustration 5-26), patterns (Illustration 5-27), and headdresses (Illustration 5-28). Encourage discussion: Which masks seem to be square? Triangular? Which masks have square and triangular shapes? Which masks have circles and rectangles? Which masks seem to be smooth? Which masks have patterns and designs?

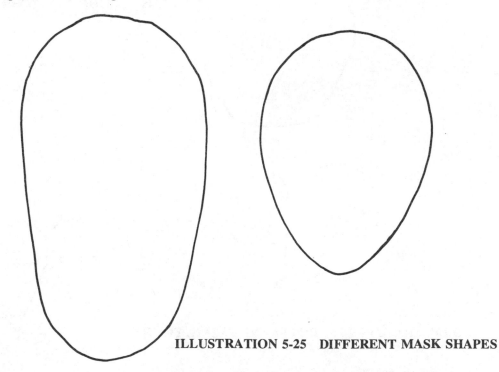

**ILLUSTRATION 5-25   DIFFERENT MASK SHAPES**

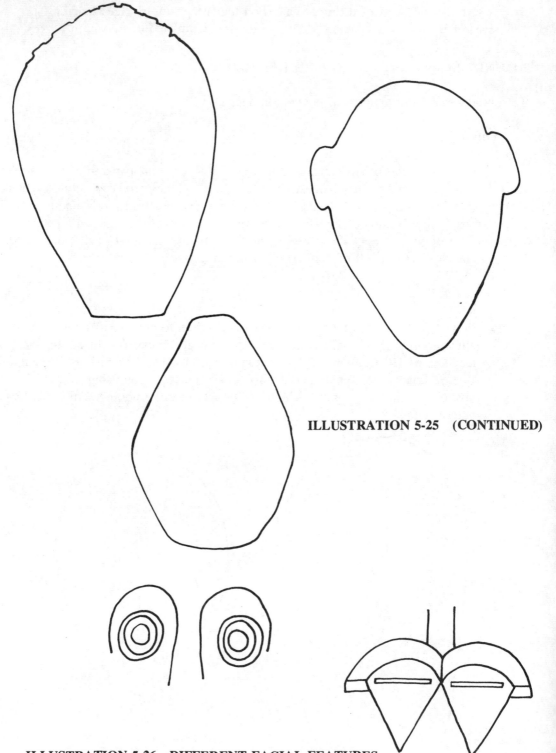

**ILLUSTRATION 5-25    (CONTINUED)**

**ILLUSTRATION 5-26    DIFFERENT FACIAL FEATURES**

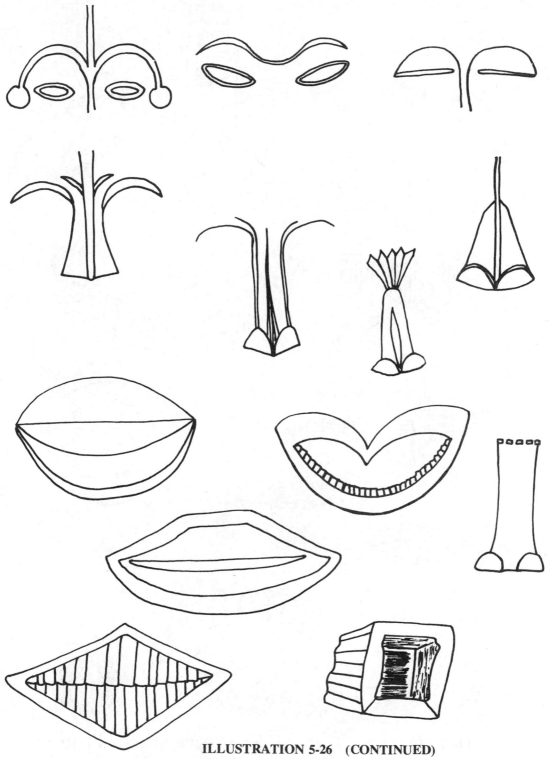

**ILLUSTRATION 5-26   (CONTINUED)**

**ILLUSTRATION 5-27    DIFFERENT PATTERNS FROM AFRICAN DESIGN**

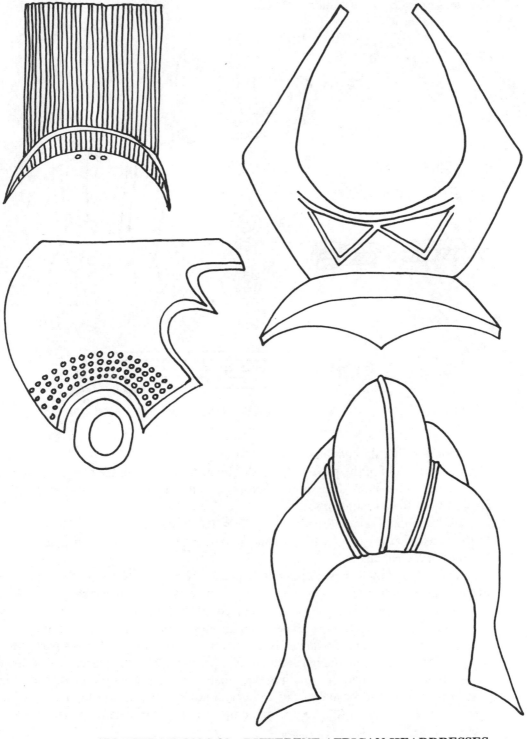

**ILLUSTRATION 5-28   DIFFERENT AFRICAN HEADDRESSES**

- Draw these patterns (Illustration 5-29) on the chalkboard. Compare them with patterns in the reproductions.

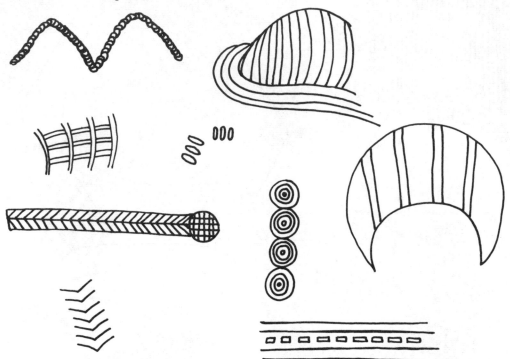

**ILLUSTRATION 5-29   AFRICAN PATTERNS FOR COMPARISON**

- Have children fold the manila paper in half lengthwise.
- Starting on the fold of the paper, cut a half circle. *Note:* Encourage children to cut a large shape. Some individuals may want to cut out the shape again if they are not satisfied with their first efforts.
- Have children each select a sheet of the 9″ × 12″ construction paper.
- On the construction paper, draw around the unfolded circle shape with crayon.
- Cut out the traced shape.
- Have children cut eyes, nose, and mouth shapes from the felt scraps.
- Arrange and paste the felt features on the circular construction paper shape to create a mask. *Note:* Emphasis should not be placed on facial expressions. The African artist expressed deep emotional experiences in his work (religious and/or magical) which grew out of psychological needs. The expression is not facial, but a part of the complete work of art. Encourage children to experiment with the placement of these felt features, for example: leave a large or small space between the eyes, slant the eyes, or place them horizontally. The forehead may become high or low, depending upon placement of eyes. A large or small chin area is determined by position of the mouth.
- Draw crayon line patterns on areas of the masks and trace over the lines to make them heavy and to make the colors stronger. (See Illustration 5-30.) *Note:* Encour-

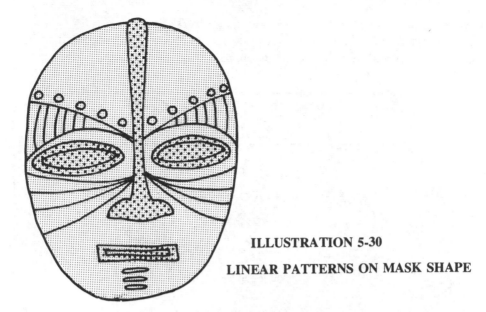

**ILLUSTRATION 5-30**

**LINEAR PATTERNS ON MASK SHAPE**

age children to consider the patterns drawn on the chalkboard, patterns on their papers from "Before You Begin" activity, and patterns on the mask prints.

- Place the five sheets of black construction paper lengthwise in a row, overlapping and pasting about 2″ where sides meet. Tape this panel of paper (or the kraft paper if used instead of the construction paper) to the chalkboard.
- Cover the backs of the finished masks with paste and press the masks on the panel. (See Illustration 5-31.) *Note:* Avoid placing them all on the same level. With supervision, children may help paste their masks on the panel.

**ILLUSTRATION 5-31**
**ROUND MASKS GROUPING**

*Can You Imagine . . .*

Do all felt masks, instead of using construction paper and felt.

Paste two masks back to back and hang as mobiles.

Cover a carton with black paper and paste masks on the four sides to display. Make a stand-up sign and place it on the top of the carton. (See Illustration 5-32.)

**ILLUSTRATION 5-32   MASK COVERED CARTON**

## MASKS INSEPARABLE (GRADES 3-4)

To arrange several shapes in a way that each shape is dependent upon another for its completion.

*You'll Need . . .*

African art books (optional, see ''Before You Begin'') • prints of African masks • manila paper 9″ × 12″ • crayons • white, beige, yellow, and orange construction paper 9″ × 24″ (1 color of each child's choice) • children's papers from ''Before You Begin'' activity • facial tissues.

*Procedures . . .*

- Have children browse through the African art books to observe the masks. Display four or five prints that show variations of African masks. Mention briefly purposes for which masks were designed (death, sickness, spiritual needs, societies, or secret organizations). Discuss surfaces of the masks and the patterns.
- Have children fold the manila paper in half lengthwise and in half widthwise.
- In each of the four spaces draw with crayon a different pattern from the African masks displayed in the prints and books. (See Illustration 5-33.)
- *In the top left space on the reverse side of the paper*, draw a crayon mask shape. (See Illustration 5-34A.)

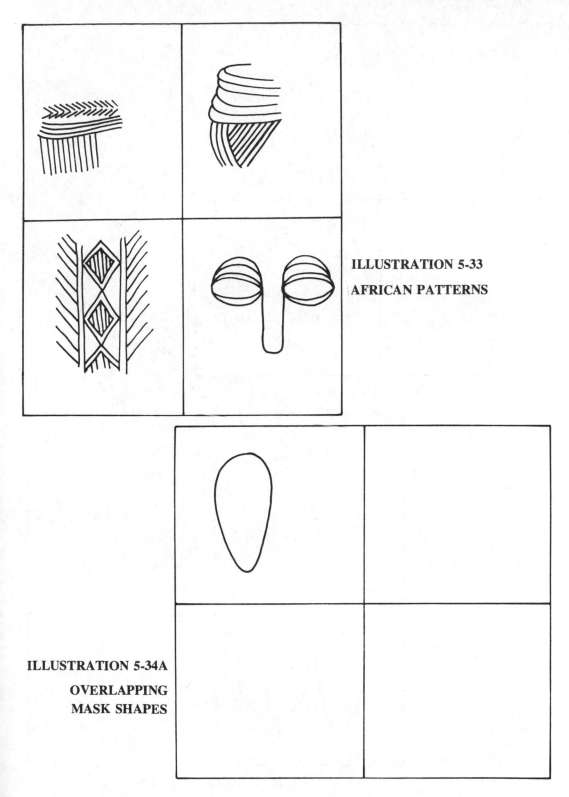

ILLUSTRATION 5-33
AFRICAN PATTERNS

ILLUSTRATION 5-34A
OVERLAPPING
MASK SHAPES

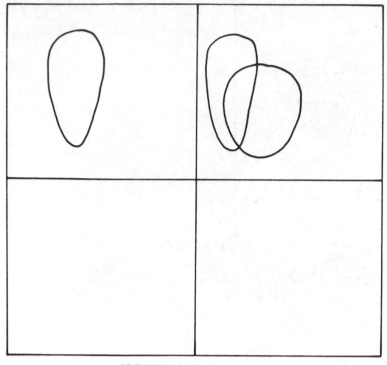

**ILLUSTRATION 5-34B**

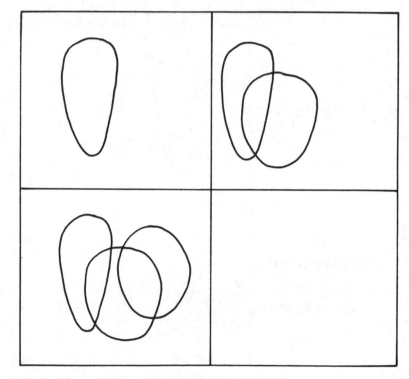

**ILLUSTRATION 5-34C**

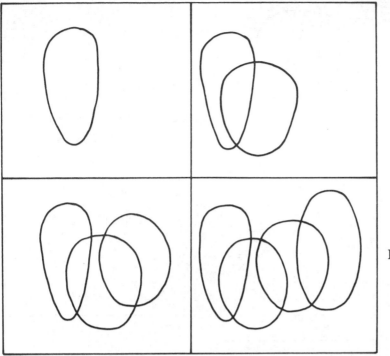

**ILLUSTRATION 5-34D**

- *In the top right space*, repeat the drawing of the first mask and draw a second mask shape that partially overlaps the first in that space. (See Illustration 5-34B.) *Note:* This shape need not be exactly identical in size or shape with the first one.
- Repeat the two overlapping mask shapes *in the bottom left space* and add a third shape that overlaps the second shape in that space. (See Illustration 5-34C.)
- *In the last space*, repeat the drawing of the three shapes and add one shape that overlaps the third shape. (See Illustration 5-34D.) *Note:* Explain that these shapes represent masks. Since the masks overlap, three eye shapes would provide eyes for two masks. Make a drawing on the chalkboard to demonstrate. (See Illustration 5-35A.) In like manner, two more eye shapes would provide the second eye for the third mask and eyes for the last mask on the right. (See Illustration 5-35B.)
- Draw crayon eye shapes on the mask shapes in the bottom right space on the paper.
- On the construction paper of their choice of color, have children draw with one color of crayon five to seven overlapping mask shapes.
- With the color of crayon used to make the mask shapes, draw eyes, nose, and mouth on each shape. *Note:* Remind children that each mask "shares an eye" as is shown in Illustration 5-36A. Encourage them to refer to eyes on the masks in the last space of their practice manila paper.
- With the same color of crayon used for the shapes and features, draw linear patterns, poles or necks, ears, and headdresses on the masks, treating each mask individually. (See Illustration 5-36B.) *Note:* Have children refer to and use some linear patterns on their papers from "Before You Begin" activity, and linear patterns drawn on the folded manila paper during the beginning procedures of this project. Encourage

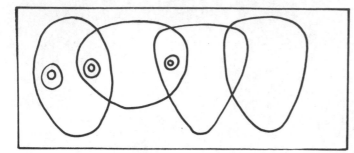

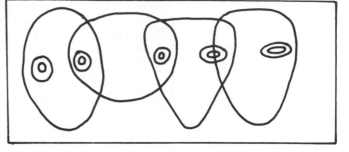

**ILLUSTRATION 5-35A**

**PLACING EYE SHAPES IN OVERLAPPING MASKS**

**ILLUSTRATION 5-35B**

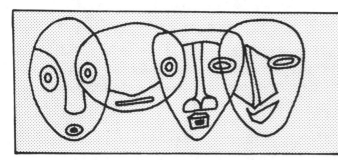

**ILLUSTRATION 5-36A**

**MASKS INSEPARABLE**

**ILLUSTRATION 5-36B**

children to consider patterns for the mask on either side of a mask on which they are drawing a pattern.

- Trace over the lines of the composition with the crayon to make them definite.
- Cover the areas between lines with heavy coats of warm or cool colors of crayon. (See Chapter 2.) *Note:* Remind children that reds, oranges, and yellows are generally warm. Blues, greens, and violets are basically cool.

- Polish the composition with a tissue. *Note:* Retrace original lines of the drawing if necessary to achieve a definite pattern.

### Can You Imagine . . .

Draw mask shapes, facial features, headdresses, poles, and linear patterns with black crayon. Paint the areas between the lines with warm or cool colors of thin tempera paint.

With black felt markers, draw "Masks Inseparable" on stark white construction paper.

Roll each completed strip into a cylinder shape. Staple the cylinder and use individually or in groups on a library table, shelves, and in corners.

## MASK REFLECTIONS (GRADES 5-6)

To create a composition of pattern repetition involving linear design.

### You'll Need . . .

Prints of African masks (see "Before You Begin") • manila paper 9″ × 12″ • crayons (3 colors of each child's choice) • cardboard 9″ × 12″ (2 per child) • scissors • children's papers from "Before You Begin" activity • paste • paste dabbers or brushes • manila drawing paper 18″ × 24″ or tracing paper.

### Procedures . . .

- Display prints of African masks. Discuss and compare the masks. Encourage detail observation by discussing basic shapes (dome, pyramid, cube, etc.), surface texture, pattern composition (curved or straight lines), number of patterns on each mask, and type of headdress (height, design, shape, etc.). *Note:* Children should be encouraged to read about the part of Africa from which a mask came, how the mask was used, etc.
- Fold the 9″ × 12″ manila paper in half lengthwise and in half widthwise.
- In each space on the paper draw a different crayon sample of the patterns seen on the various masks.
- *On the reverse side* of the folded paper, draw a crayoned mask shape *in the top left space.* (See Illustration 5-37A.)
- *In the top right space*, repeat the mask shape and add facial features as suggested in Illustration 5-37B.
- *In the bottom left space*, repeat the drawing from the second space and add details to enhance or change the drawing. (See Illustration 5-37C.)
- *In the bottom right space*, repeat the drawing from the third space and add headdress, pole, ears, etc. (See Illustration 5-37D.)
- Draw a mask shape on one piece of the cardboard. *Note:* The shape should be at least seven or eight inches in height. Headdress, pole, and ears may be included in this drawing if desired. Have children use their drawings on manila paper as reference.
- Cut out the mask shape.

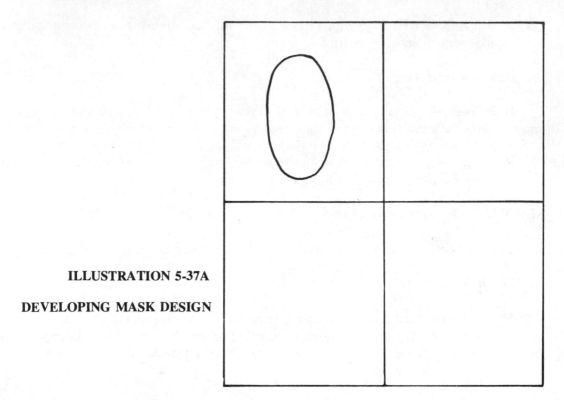

**ILLUSTRATION 5-37A**

**DEVELOPING MASK DESIGN**

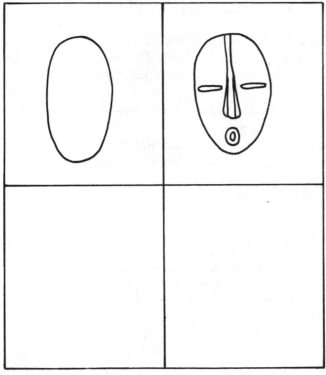

**ILLUSTRATION 5-37B**

**ILLUSTRATION 5-37C**

**ILLUSTRATION 5-37D**

- With the color of crayon used for the mask shape, draw eyes, nose, and mouth shapes on the cardboard mask.
- With the same color of crayon, draw patterns on the cardboard mask (Illustration 5-38A) after considering the following: shape of mask (and headdress if there is one), type of line best suited for the mask shape (curved, straight, etc.), number of patterns to be used (one or more), and placement of pattern or patterns. *Note:* Encourage children to refer to and use some linear patterns from ''Before You Begin'' activity, and linear patterns drawn on the manila paper during the beginning procedures of this project.
- Cut out and paste cardboard eyes, nose, and mouth shapes on top of the crayoned facial features on the cardboard mask. (See Illustration 5-38B.) *Note:* Shapes need not be the same size as the crayoned features.

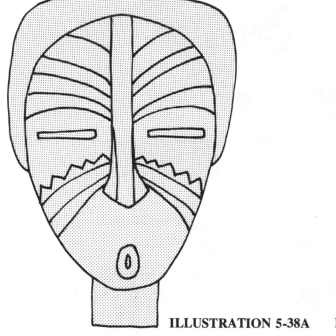

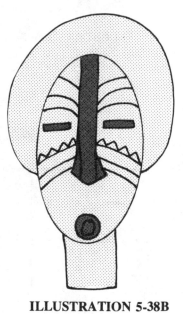

**ILLUSTRATION 5-38B**

**ILLUSTRATION 5-38A     RAISED FEATURES**

- Cut out and paste a cardboard headdress shape on the mask.
- Cut and paste thin strips of cardboard of different lengths on the crayoned lines that form linear patterns on the mask.
- Place the 18″ × 24″ manila drawing paper or tracing paper over the cardboard mask.
- With the side of one unwrapped piece of crayon, rub over the paper until the complete mask image with patterns is reproduced on the paper. (See Illustration 5-39A.) *Note:* Crayon of about 3″ in length works best for the rubbing. The paper should be held carefully so that it and the mask do not shift positions.
- Without moving the mask or the paper, repeat the rubbing process with a second color.

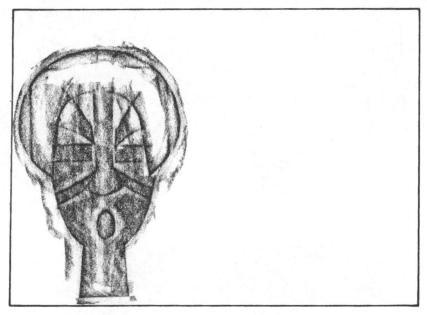

**ILLUSTRATION 5-39A**

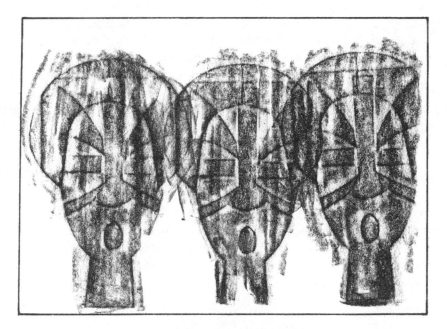

**ILLUSTRATION 5-39B**
**MASK   REFLECTIONS**

- Move the mask to a new position under the manila drawing paper and make another rubbing, using both colors.

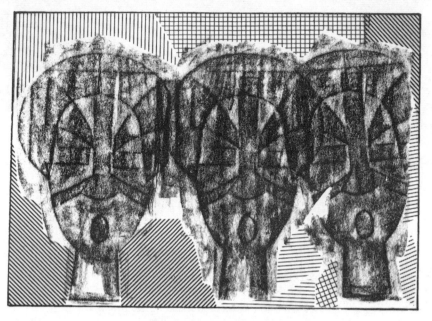

**ILLUSTRATION 5-39C**

- Continue to repeat this procedure until the paper is covered with mask rubbings. (See Illustration 5-39B.) *Note:* Remove the cardboard mask from the desk.
- Select one of the linear patterns from ''Before You Begin'' activity or from the small folded manila paper used during the beginning procedures of this project.
- With one of the colors (except yellow) used for the rubbings, draw the selected pattern in the spaces around the mask rubbings. (See Illustration 5-39C.) *Note:* A successful project results from: varying widths and lengths of the strips pasted on the cardboard mask shape, holding the paper and mask perfectly still while rubbing with crayon, and applying even pressure to the crayon while rubbing.

*Can You Imagine . . .*

Paint over the whole mask composition with a water color.

Make rubbings on tissue and use it as wrapping paper for a gift.

After making the mask rubbings on the manila drawing paper or tracing paper, paste thin strips of construction paper of one color on the lines of the designs. Use the same color of crayon to make the patterns in spaces around the masks.

# CHAPTER 6

# SHAPES AROUND YOU

Anything created by nature or made by man has the basic form of a circle, square, or triangle. This chapter provides opportunities for children to use distortion, repetition, and combinations of these geometric shapes in a variety of arrangements. To further emphasize the importance of shape in composition, children will analyze works of master painters. When children begin to notice concrete and imaginary shapes around them, then they are developing perception, learning to see detail in composition, and building visual and tactile experiences that will give strength and meaning to their own creative two- and three-dimensional compositions.

## BEFORE YOU BEGIN

Start the children "thinking in shapes." On a table, display an apple, a banana, a pear, and a bunch of grapes and discuss their shapes. The apple is representative of the circle (Figure 6-1) and the banana has the shape of a circle variation, that is, a long oval (Figure 6-2). Figure 6-3 shows the formation of a pear from two circles, a small circle gently

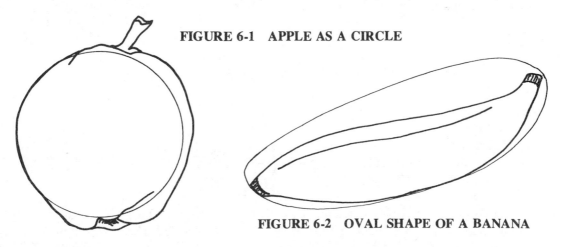

FIGURE 6-1   APPLE AS A CIRCLE

FIGURE 6-2   OVAL SHAPE OF A BANANA

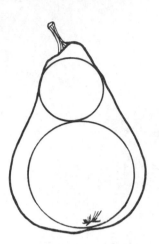

**FIGURE 6-3   THE PEAR AS CIRCLES**

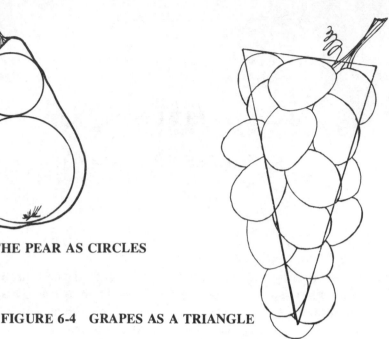

**FIGURE 6-4   GRAPES AS A TRIANGLE**

merging into a large circle. Or, is it one oval? A bunch of grapes is one large triangle shaped by repetition of overlapping groups of small ovals (Figure 6-4).

Ask the class to take a "seeing tour" around the room and try to identify objects as being basic variations of a circle, square, or triangle. What shapes were used to create the desk, chair, floor pattern, light fixtures, etc.?

It is important for children to understand that no matter the extent of distortion or variation of a shape, the basic characteristics of the shape remain the same.

For example, the basic characteristics (four sides) of this distorted figure are those of a square.

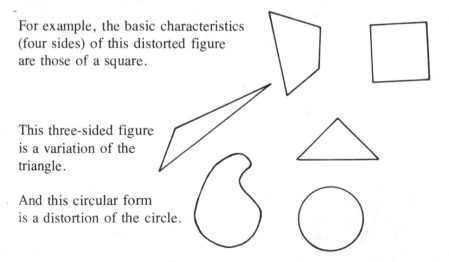

This three-sided figure is a variation of the triangle.

And this circular form is a distortion of the circle.

What shapes are involved in the human body? With a rectangular piece of paper, show that it becomes a three-dimensional cylindrical shape when rolled. (See Figures 6-5A and

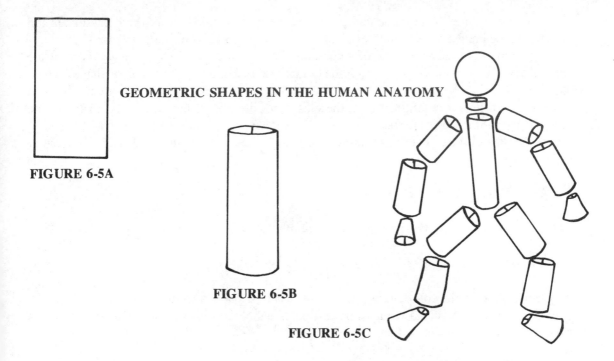

**GEOMETRIC SHAPES IN THE HUMAN ANATOMY**

**FIGURE 6-5A**

**FIGURE 6-5B**

**FIGURE 6-5C**

6-5B.) Ask a child to stand in front of the class. Note that the body is made up basically of these rectangles or square *variations*, plus a circular shape (Figure 6-5C).

Display leaves of different shapes on a bulletin board. Help the children discuss and see that a leaf can be a distortion of the circle, triangle, or square. (See Figure 6-6.)

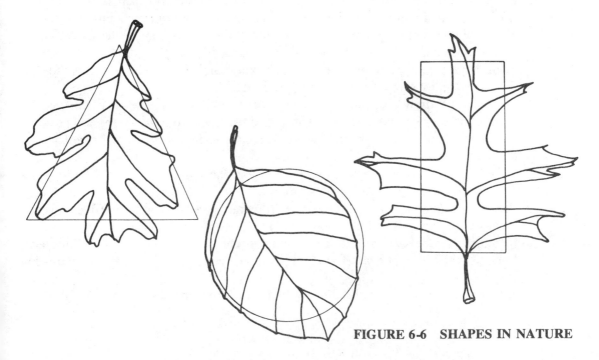

**FIGURE 6-6   SHAPES IN NATURE**

Ask the children to examine patterned clothing (prints and knits) of their classmates and identify shapes and combinations of shapes which are repeated in the patterns.

Challenge the class to think of something that is not derived from one or more of the basic shapes. If a response is given, guide children in discovering the shape or shapes. Have old magazines available so that a child may look for a picture of the object to display and analyze. If an object mentioned is in the classroom or school, have the class examine the item for its geometric properties.

When the children begin "thinking in shapes," they will begin to exhibit more creativity.

## A CIRCLE MOBILE (GRADES K-2)

To use a variety of geometric shapes on a circular form.

*You'll Need . . .*

Scissors • bright colors of 9″ × 12″ construction paper (1 color per child's choice) • crayons (except yellow and white) • paste • paste dabbers or brushes • 1 pair of punchers • yarn (many colors or one color).

*Procedures . . .*

- Have children watch as you cut a large freehand circle from a piece of construction paper. Identify the shape and talk about things that are circular.
- Have children cut a large freehand circle from their construction paper. *Note:* Perfection of shape is not necessary as long as the shape approximates a circle.
- Have children write their first names with crayon on one side of the circle. *Note:* Assist those children who cannot write independently.
- Collect the scraps of colored construction paper and have children select three or four that are not the same color as their circles.
- On the board draw a square and triangle for the children. Identify each shape.
- Have children cut small circles, squares, and triangles from the scraps and paste on the other side of their paper circle. *Note:* Have them leave space between and around the small shapes.
- Draw crayon circles, squares, and triangles in the spaces, filling the large paper circle with these shapes. (See Illustration 6-1A.)
- Punch two holes in each child's circle (Illustration 6-1B) and string five to seven circles with yarn. (See Illustration 6-1C.)
- Knot the yarn before and after each circle so that the shapes will remain in place. *Note:* A yarn or paper tassel at the bottom of the mobile provides an interesting touch.
- Attach circle mobiles overhead in an area away from the wall.

**A CIRCLE MOBILE**

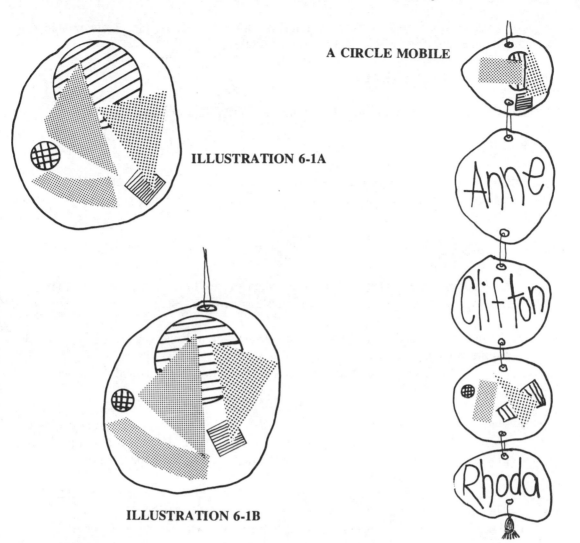

ILLUSTRATION 6-1A

ILLUSTRATION 6-1B

ILLUSTRATION 6-1C

*Can You Imagine . . .*

Have children draw or cut out magazine pictures of a few of "their favorite things." Instead of cutting around the exact configuration of a picture, have children cut around it so that it is contained within a circular shape. Paste the pictures on other large circles of construction paper. String these as mobiles.

On one side of the circle, make shapes to represent funny, crayon facial features or paste on features made from shapes cut from paper scraps. Attach yarn hair to the funny faces. Add one or more faces to each of the circle mobiles.

Make "A Square Mobile" and "A Triangle Mobile," using the general procedures suggested for "A Circle Mobile."

On a colorful background, make a mural of animals, people, and plants created from circles. Intersperse different sizes and colors of circles.

## LEAVES AND LINES (GRADES 3-4)

To create a composition involving shape repetition and linear design.

*You'll Need . . .*

Pressed leaves that suggest at least two basic shapes • crayons • construction paper scraps (a little larger than the leaves) • scissors • pastel construction paper 12″ × 18″ (or larger).

*Procedures . . .*

*Note:* To press the leaves, put them between pieces of waxed paper and then between pages of a book two or three days prior to the lesson.

- Spread the pressed leaves on a table. Discuss their basic shapes, sizes, etc. (See Figure 6-6, page 179.)
- Have children each select a leaf and, with crayon, trace around it on a scrap of construction paper.
- Cut out the traced leaf, being careful to follow the true leaf outline.
- On the pastel construction paper, repeatedly trace around the paper leaf to illustrate falling, floating leaves. (See Illustration 6-2A.) *Note:* For each tracing, children place the leaf in a different direction on a new area of the paper. Some leaf shapes should touch the four edges of the paper.
- Extend all leaf stems to the edges of the paper as shown in Illustration 6-2B. *Note:* The stems may appear to pass under or over the leaf shapes.
- With the same color of crayon used for drawing around the leaf patterns, fill in empty areas with line designs (Illustration 6-2C). *Note:* Refer to line design in Chapter 4.

**ILLUSTRATION 6-2A**

**ILLUSTRATION 6-2B**

**ILLUSTRATION 6-2C**
**LEAVES AND LINES**

- Add more color to the composition by selecting two different colors of crayon and blending them within the leaf shapes.

*Can You Imagine . . .*

Make the composition of "Leaves and Lines" by tracing heavy with white waxed crayon around the leaf pattern on black construction paper. Fill in areas with line designs, using the white crayon.

Use yellow crayon on white paper to create the composition of "Leaves and Lines." Paint with water colors between the crayoned lines. In order for this approach to be successful, the crayoned leaf outlines and lines must be drawn heavily.

On scrap cloth, trace around the leaf pattern. Cut out cloth leaves and paste on burlap, allowing some of them to overlap. Add yarn stems and string veins.

## REPEAT THAT SHAPE (GRADES 5-6)

To use circular shape dominance in composition.

*You'll Need . . .*

Print of Pierre Renoir's *Madame Renoir* • manila paper 9″ × 12″ • pencils • manila drawing paper strips 6″ × 24″ • felt markers or crayons.

*Procedures . . .*

- Draw a circle shape (about 8″ in diameter) slowly on the chalkboard. Mention that the shape is a curved line. (See Chapter 4.) Draw an oval shape on the board. Remind the class that this shape is a curved line, too, and is a variation of the circle. Explain that many compositions when analyzed will reveal a basic shape dominance.
- Display the print. With the pointer, trace around the head and hat of Madame Renoir, noting the overlapping of the two circular shapes. (See Illustration 6-3A.) Ask children to observe the shape of Madame Renoir's upper torso. This shape is created by an invisible line that connects the shoulders, outlines the arms and is completed by the overlapping hands of the figure. With the pointer, trace this circular shape of the upper torso. (See Illustration 6-3B.) Help children note that

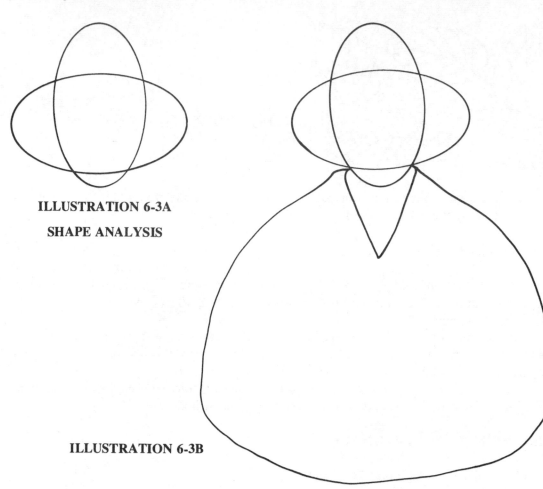

**ILLUSTRATION 6-3A**

**SHAPE ANALYSIS**

**ILLUSTRATION 6-3B**

Renoir has repeated this circular shape again in the form of two flowers on the hat, the color on each cheek, the button on the blouse, and the earring. (See Illustration 6-3C.) Observe that the rounded fullness of the upper torso is achieved through the use of color also.

- Have children fold the 9" × 12" manila paper into four equal parts.
- *In the first box* (or part), with a pencil do a circular analysis of the head and hat as shown in Illustration 6-4A.
- *In the second box*, do a circular analysis of the body. (See Illustration 6-4B.)
- Combine the head and hat and body analyses *in the third box* as suggested in Illustration 6-4C.
- *In the fourth box*, alter the drawing described for the third box by changing the size relationship of the circular shapes to each other. *Note:* For example: Enlarge the hat shape; reduce the size of the head; enlarge the cheek shapes, earring, one flower; and reduce the size of the button and body torso. (See Illustration 6-4D.)
- *In each box on back of the paper*, experiment with varying sizes of circular shapes as suggested in Illustration 6-5.

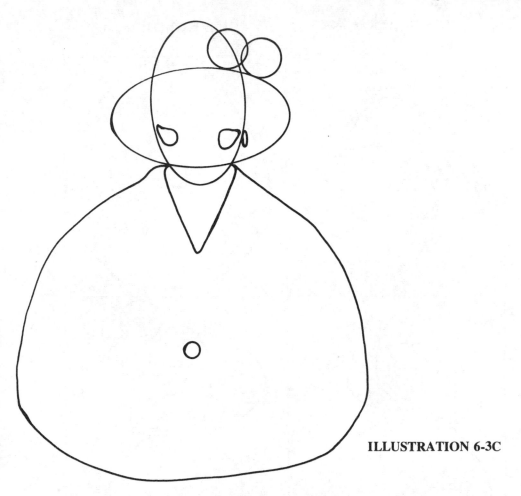

**ILLUSTRATION 6-3C**

- Select one of the last five arrangements (Illustrations 6-4D and 6-5) that involve changes in the size relationships of the circular shapes.
- Fold the 6″ × 24″ manila paper strip into four 6″ wide sections and make a pencilled copy of the selected arrangement in the first space. (See Illustration 6-6A.) *Note:* Encourage children to fill the space with the drawing.
- Repeat this drawing in the other three spaces.
- Across each fold draw a circular shape that overlaps the drawing on either side of the fold as shown in Illustration 6-6B. *Note:* Remind children that they will draw three of these shapes because there are three folds.
- Trace over all the lines with the felt marker or crayon. *Note:* To enhance this composition, firm, strong, and steady lines should be used when tracing.

*Can You Imagine . . .*

Use the procedures with one or more of the following prints: Franz Marc's *Blue Horses,* and *The Sheep*, and Vincent Van Gogh's *Starry Nite*.

ILLUSTRATION 6-4A                    ILLUSTRATION 6-4B

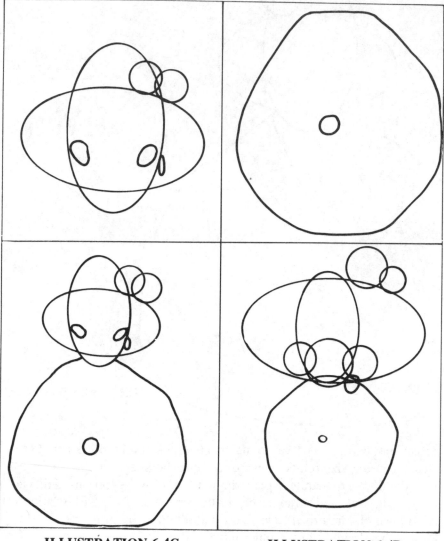

ILLUSTRATION 6-4C                    ILLUSTRATION 6-4D

## EXPERIMENTING WITH CIRCULAR SHAPE ANALYSIS

With a different color of crayon, color each new shape formed by overlapping shapes in the first panel section. Repeat the colors in the other sections.

With a pencil copy the selected arrangement on paper towelling three or more times. Trace over the lines with crayon. Fill in the areas with pastel felt markers.

## SEEING CIRCLES IN COMPOSITION (GRADES K-2)

To create a composition in which a geometric shape dominates.

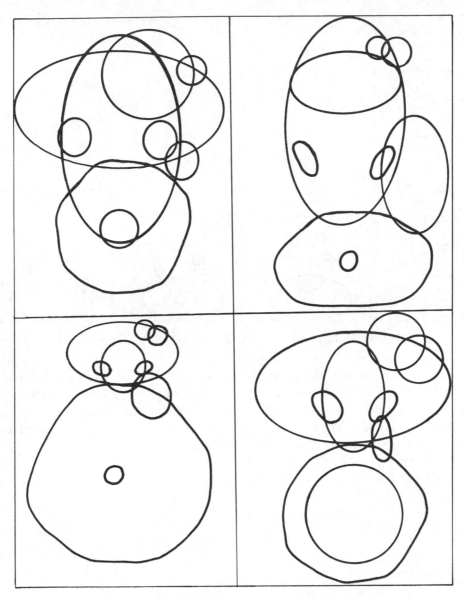

**ILLUSTRATION 6-5   VARYING TOTAL SHAPE ANALYSIS**

*You'll Need . . .*

A print of Vincent Van Gogh's *Sunflowers* • two 4″ construction paper circles of different colors • crayons • manila drawing paper 9″ × 12″.

*Procedures . . .*

• Display Van Gogh's *Sunflowers*. Draw a circle (about 5″ in diameter) on the board.

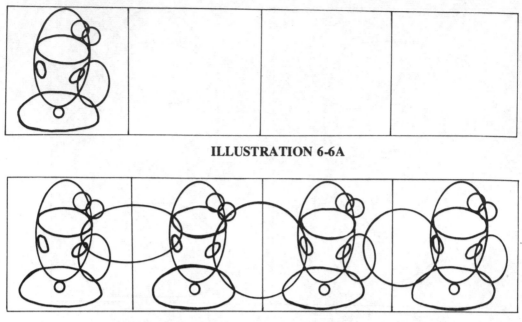

**ILLUSTRATION 6-6A**

**ILLUSTRATION 6-6B    PANEL OF REPEATED SHAPES**

With the pointer follow along the edge of one of the flower shapes in the painting. Ask the children why this shape reminds them of the circle on the chalkboard.

- Have several children use the pointer to identify other circular shapes in the painting. Point to the circular shapes that are partially hidden by other circles. Explain that these circular shapes are still complete although all of each one can not be seen.
- Demonstrate this by partially covering one construction paper circle with the other. (See Illustration 6-7A.) While holding the shapes in this manner, turn them around

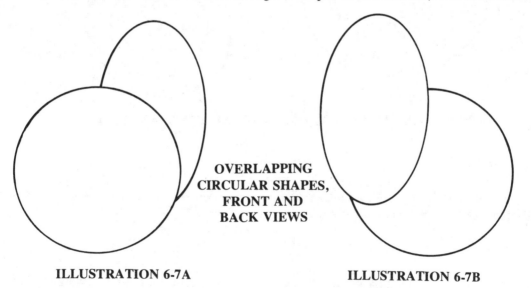

**OVERLAPPING CIRCULAR SHAPES, FRONT AND BACK VIEWS**

**ILLUSTRATION 6-7A**                    **ILLUSTRATION 6-7B**

or over so the back can be seen. (See Illustration 6-7B.) Explain that both circles remain whole even though one is partially hidden.

- While holding the circles in this overlapping position, have a child point out in the painting two circular shapes that are similar in the arrangement shown.
- On the manila paper, have children make crayon circles in the arrangement seen in the Van Gogh print. *Note:* Use only one color of crayon for the drawing.
- Add crayon leaves and vase. (See Illustration 6-8.)

**ILLUSTRATION 6-8   FREE SKETCH OF SUNFLOWERS**

- Color the composition with various colors of crayon, using a circular movement to apply the color.
- Color the background by blending the crayons so that colors show through other colors. *Note:* Have children apply the crayon using circular movements.

*Can You Imagine . . .*

Free cut the circular shapes from scraps of construction paper. Paste them on bogus. Complete the picture by adding crayoned leaves and flower centers.

Use round color patches cut from magazine to reconstruct a composition similar to the one in Van Gogh's painting.

With one color of crayon draw the composition on a sheet of the newspaper want ad section. Add tempera paint to various areas.

Use the procedures with one or more of the following prints: Pablo Picasso's *Fruit and Wine Glass*, Gustave Courbet's *Still Life, Apples and Pomegranates*, Paul Cezanne's *Still Life with Apples and Oranges*.

## KEEP YOUR EYE ON THE CIRCLE (GRADES 3-4)

To create a composition by which circular shapes appear fused with other shapes in a composition, yet remain independent of each other.

*You'll Need . . .*

A print of Paul Klee's *Dynamism of a Head* • 5 pieces of chalk of different colors that appear bright when used on the chalkboard • 18″ drawing paper circular shapes • crayons (black only) • 3 or more colors of tissue paper pieces 9″ × 12″ (5 sheets per child, 3 colors per child) • scissors • paste • paste dabbers or brushes.

*Procedures . . .*

- Display Klee's *Dynamism of a Head*. Encourage the class to comment on the color usage in this composition. (See Chapter 2 on color.) Ask the children to tell how many circular shapes they see in the composition. On the board draw the shapes shown in Illustration 6-9. Draw each with a different color of chalk. Keep the size

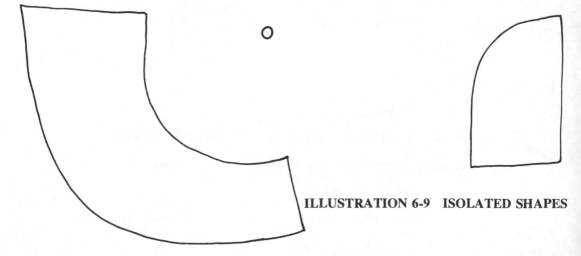

**ILLUSTRATION 6-9   ISOLATED SHAPES**

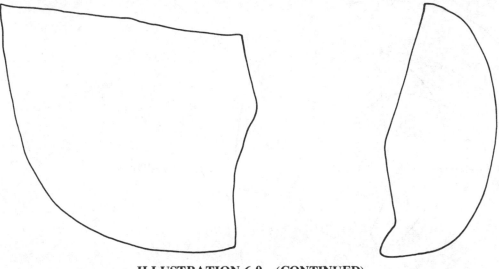

**ILLUSTRATION 6-9   (CONTINUED)**

relationship about the same as pictured. Have children identify these shapes in the composition of the print by tracing around the edge of each shape with a pointer. Explain that every circle is involved with another. That is, if any circle is removed, then a portion of another circle is removed also.

- On the drawing paper, have children reproduce crayon circular shapes that appear in the print (Illustration 6-10A).

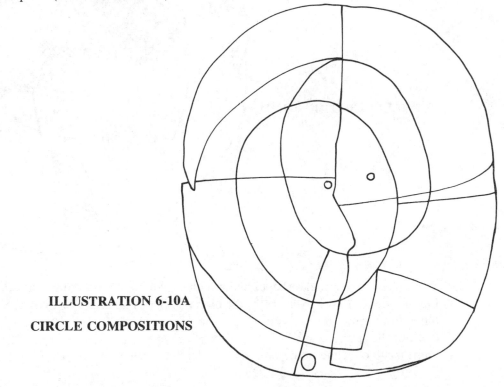

**ILLUSTRATION 6-10A**

**CIRCLE COMPOSITIONS**

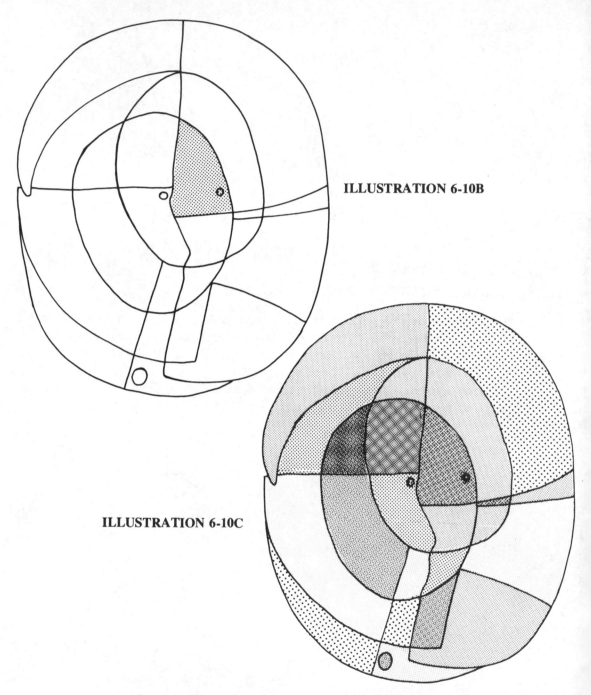

ILLUSTRATION 6-10B

ILLUSTRATION 6-10C

- Trace over these circular shapes again with crayon to make the lines thick and dark.
- Lay a sheet of tissue over one of the circular shapes and trace with crayon the shape that shows through the tissue.
- Cut out the tissue shape.
- Paint paste over the entire area of the identical shape on the paper circle.

- Carefully smooth the matching tissue shape onto the paste covered area (Illustration 6-10B). *Note:* Remind children to smooth out all wrinkles and paste down corners.
- Trace, cut out, and paste tissue shapes on the other circular shapes. *Note:* Have children use scraps of a tissue sheet for smaller shapes. If a shape overlaps a previously pasted-on shape, put paste also over the area where the overlap occurs. (See Illustration 6-10C.) If a shape has been drawn heavily, it should remain visible through another tissue shape that overlaps it. In some areas there may be as many as three layers of tissue, or as few as one. Have children note that new colors are created as one color of tissue is pasted over another.

### Can You Imagine . . .

Use some of the tissue shapes as patterns. Trace around them on newspaper. Cut out the newspaper shapes. Combine the newspaper and tissue shapes to create Klee's composition.

Instead of tissue paper, substitute corrugated cardboard turned in various directions to create varied linear designs.

With crayon on a 12″ square of manila paper, draw all the circular shapes in the arrangement used in the print. Cut out each shape. Arrange and paste the shapes in a different composition on a 12″ square of colored construction paper. Color the different shapes with various colors of crayon.

Use the procedures with one or more of the following prints: Robert Delaunay's *Homage to Bleroit,* and *Simultaneous Disk,* and Franz Marc's *Tower of Blue Horses*.

## DISTORTING THE BIRD (GRADES 5-6)

To experiment with distorting selected forms to fit a precut shape.

### You'll Need . . .

Prints of cubistic works by Braque and Picasso, and prints of works by Dali • manila paper 9″ × 12″ • pencils • scissors • pastel construction paper 9″ × 12″ • crayons • paste • paste dabbers or brushes • pastel construction paper 12″ × 18″.

### Procedures . . .

- Discuss the meaning of *distortion*. Display the prints. Have children observe that Braque and Picasso seem to rearrange the basic geometric shapes so that it is possible to view several angles of a subject at one time. Dali seems to stretch and melt his subject matter.
- On the manila paper, have children make a very simple, pencilled drawing of a bird (Illustration 6-11).
- On the back of the manila paper, draw sample distortions of the bird as suggested in Illustration 6-12. *Note:* Encourage children to make birds of different sizes, tall and thin, short and wide, long and narrow, etc.

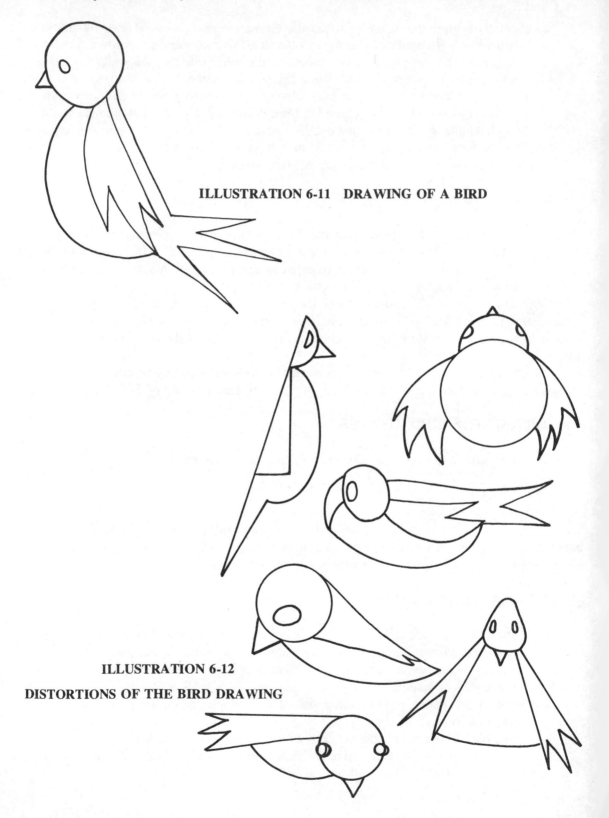

**ILLUSTRATION 6-11  DRAWING OF A BIRD**

**ILLUSTRATION 6-12**

**DISTORTIONS OF THE BIRD DRAWING**

- Cut the 9″ × 12″ construction paper into three parts by making only two cuts. *Note:* Different ways of cutting the paper are suggested in Illustration 6-13.

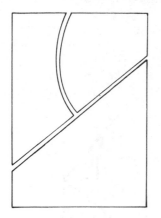
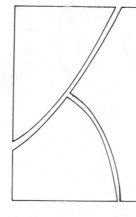
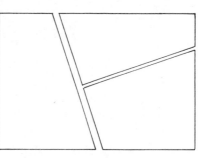

**ILLUSTRATION 6-13**
**DIVIDING THE RECTANGLE**

- On one of the three pieces of construction paper, with crayon distort a bird so that it fits the shape of the paper and occupies nearly all of the paper. (See Illustration 6-14A.) *Note:* Have children use their pencilled drawings on the manila paper as reference.
- Distort a bird on each of the two remaining pieces of cut paper. (See Illustration 6-14B.)

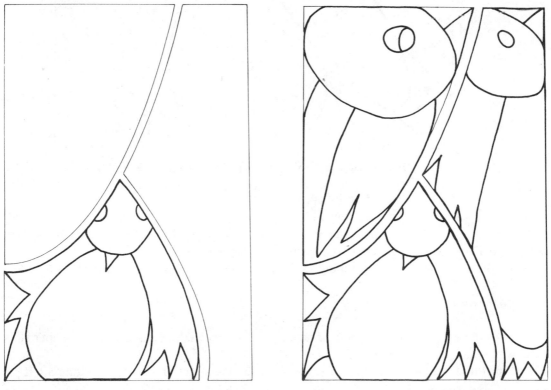

**ILLUSTRATION 6-14A**          **ILLUSTRATION 6-14B**
**FITTING THE BIRD TO THE SHAPE**

**ILLUSTRATION 6-15A   DISTORTING THE BIRD**

- Color the birds with heavily applied crayon.
- Cut away any paper surrounding the bird.
- Arrange and paste the birds on the 12″ × 18″ construction paper. (See Illustration 6-15A.) *Note:* Encourage overlapping of shapes.
- With crayon, add overlapping leaf shapes and branches. (See Illustration 6-15B.)

*Can You Imagine . . .*

Select one distorted bird cutout. Trace around it repeatedly on a rectangular paper strip. Glue tiny yarn pieces on the birds.

Substitute a paper towel for the 9″ × 12″ pastel construction paper; substitute a felt pen

**ILLUSTRATION 6-15B**

for the crayon. Carry out the procedures for "Distorting the Bird." Paste the paper towel bird shapes on 9″ × 12″ construction paper.

Do a distortion of the human figure using a black felt marker on a sheet of newspaper. Mount on gray bogus paper.

## THE SHAPE OF BUILDINGS (GRADES K-2)

To use a shape and its variation in a composition.

### *You'll Need . . .*

A large quantity of various sizes of squares and square variations (rectangles) not to exceed 4″ in length or 3″ in width, precut from corrugated cardboard, felt, construction paper, newspaper, cardboard, cloth, colorful wrapping paper, ribbon, etc. ● paste ● paste dabbers or brushes ● brown kraft paper 24″ × 10″ ● crayons.

*Procedures . . .*

- Display several different sizes of the squares and square variations as suggested in Illustration 6-16. Ask questions regarding these shapes: Which one would make the

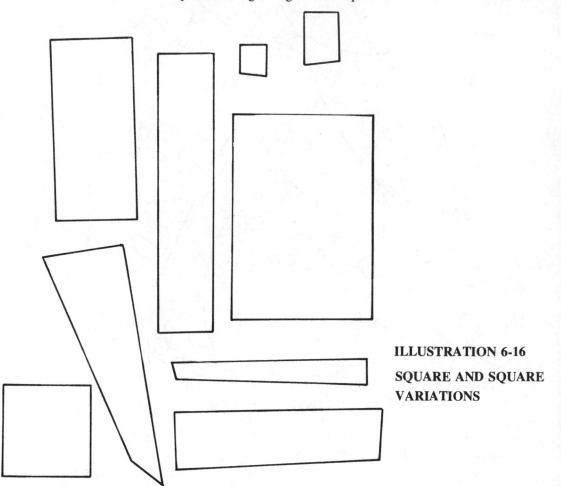

**ILLUSTRATION 6-16**

**SQUARE AND SQUARE VARIATIONS**

best building? Why? Which would make a good window? Which one could be a brick? Which one looks like a door? Talk about shapes on top of shapes. Illustrate by placing a small square or its variation on a large square variation to resemble a window or a brick on a building. (See Illustration 6-17.)
- Put a small pile of squares and square variations of different textures on the children's tables or desks.
- Have children assemble several buildings by pasting shapes on shapes as suggested in Illustration 6-18A.

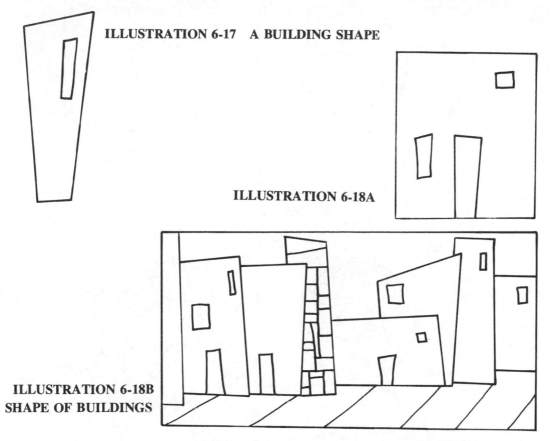

**ILLUSTRATION 6-17   A BUILDING SHAPE**

**ILLUSTRATION 6-18A**

**ILLUSTRATION 6-18B
SHAPE OF BUILDINGS**

- Paste assembled buildings on the kraft paper. *Note:* Encourage children to overlap the buildings. (See Illustration 6-18B.)
- Color in sky, ground, and sidewalks.

*Can You Imagine . . .*

Make a wall mural of children's individual buildings to depict a community.

Mount individual buildings on cardboard and attach cardboard stands. Arrange the buildings on a table to form a ''Table Town.''

Make a ''Night Scene of Buildings.'' Use only dark colors of textured rectangles. Paste assembled buildings on two or more sheets of dark blue, violet, or black construction paper taped together.

## FLOWERS BEHIND FLOWERS (GRADES 3-4)

To experiment with design variations using large and small circles.

*You'll Need . . .*

Manila paper 9″ × 12″ • crayons (4 colors per child's choice) • several pictures and

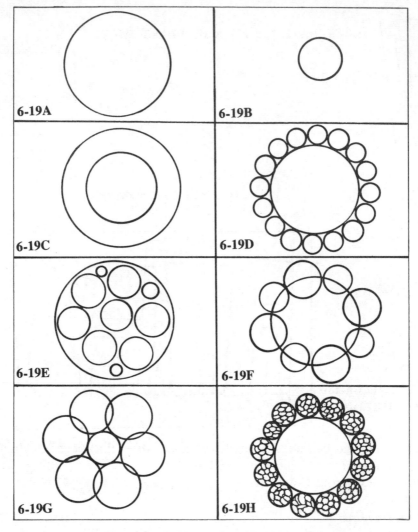

**ILLUSTRATIONS   COMBINING CIRCLE SHAPES 6-19A to 16-9H**

prints of floral arrangements (for example, *Sunflowers* by Vincent Van Gogh) • manila paper 12″ × 18″.

*Procedures . . .*

- Have children fold the manila paper once lengthwise and twice along the width.
- Place the unfolded paper on the desk vertically.
- *In the first box*, have children draw a large crayon circle (Illustration 6-19A). *Note:* Have children use only one color of crayon for drawing on this paper. Circles need not be perfect in shape; roundness is sufficient.
- *In the second box*, draw a small circle (Illustration 6-19B).

**ILLUSTRATION 6-20   COMBINING MORE CIRCLE SHAPES**

- *In the third box*, draw a small circle inside a large circle (Illustration 6-19C).
- *In the fourth box*, draw small circles that surround and touch the outer edge of a large circle. (See Illustration 6-19D.)
- *In the fifth box*, draw a large circle filled with small circles, which may or may not touch each other. (See Illustration 6-19E.)
- *In the sixth box* (Illustration 6-19F), draw small circles that surround and overlap the edge of a large circle. *Note:* The small circles need not overlap themselves.
- *In the seventh box*, draw large circles that overlap each other and that surround and touch the edge of a small circle (Illustration 6-19G).
- *In the last box*, draw small circles that surround a large circle and fill each small circle with smaller circles. (See Illustration 6-19H.)

- Have children create different arrangements by combining large and small circles in the eight boxes on the back of the folded manila paper. *Note:* See Illustration 6-20 for suggestions of other possible arrangements. Ask the children to think of their sixteen circular arrangements as flowers and to check the twelve that they find the most appealing or satisfying.
- Display pictures and prints of the floral arrangements. Discuss the positions of the flowers within the pictures. Use words such as *overlapping, behind, in front, background, far away, close*. Note that parts of some flowers are not completely visible. Also, point out that the flowers are not lined up in a row.
- Have children copy one of their twelve selected flowers in crayon anywhere, on the 12″ × 18″ manila paper, except in the center. (See Illustration 6-21A.)
- Trace over the crayon lines to make them heavy.
- Copy another flower so that it is partially hidden by the first flower. (See Illustration 6-21B.)

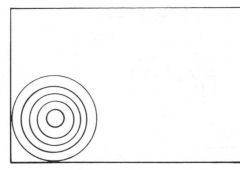

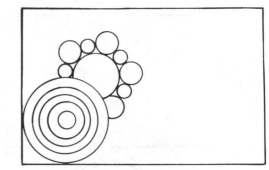

**ILLUSTRATION 6-21A**                    **ILLUSTRATION 6-21B**

**ILLUSTRATION 6-21C**

**FLOWERS BEHIND FLOWERS**

- Copy the other selected flowers so that each one is partially hidden by another. *Note:* Encourage children to fill all the spaces on the paper with overlapping flower shapes as suggested in Illustration 6-21C. In order to do this, they may add new flower shapes.
- Use three different colors (see Chapter 1 on color) of crayon to color any background space and space between flowers.

*Can You Imagine . . .*

Cover the exposed portions of window shades with the "Flowers Behind Flowers" compositions.

Paint or "wash over" the design with yellow, red, or blue water color.

Cover a large carton with the compositions to create a "Colorful Cube" for the classroom.

## SIGHTING THE INVISIBLE SPATIAL SHAPES (GRADES 5-6)

To create a composition in which shapes are inferred as the eye moves from one object to another.

*You'll Need . . .*

Two sheets of white or gray construction paper 18″ × 24″, each with black crayon drawings to resemble Illustrations 6-22 and 6-23A • crayons • prints of Ben Shahn's *Handball*, Grant Wood's *Fall Plowing*, Van Gogh's *Cafe De Nuit* • scissors • gray, black, white construction paper 12″ × 18″ (1 of each color per child) • gray bogus pieces 14″ × 16″ • paste • paste dabbers or brushes • 3 skeins each of black, gray and white yarn cut into 18″ to 20″ lengths.

*Procedures . . .*

- Display the drawing of Illustration 6-22. Ask children what the composition suggests to them. (Responses may include buildings, yard, city scene, street.) Ask what shape is dominant.
- Display the drawing of Illustration 6-23A beside the other drawing. Ask which rectangle in this second drawing is the farthest away. (The correct response is the rectangle closest to the center of the composition or rectangle number 3.) Ask how many rectangles are there in the drawing. Ask how many triangles are there. (The response may be none. However, there are 5 or more triangles.) Explain that not all shapes are obvious in a composition; some shapes may be inferred. There are at least 5 triangles inferred in Illustration 6-23A as shown in Illustration 6-23B. These are called spatial shapes. To help children become aware of these spatial shapes, make a red line from the top of rectangle 1 to the center of rectangle 3 on the drawing of Illustration 6-23A. Also draw a blue line from the center of rectangle 3 to the base

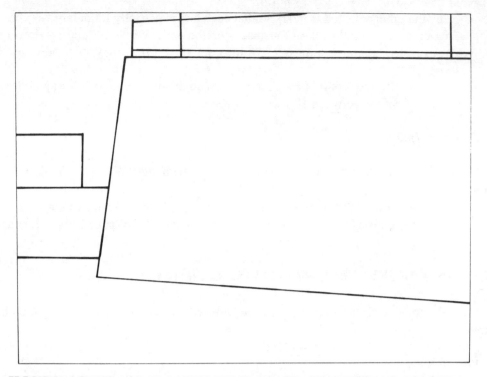

**ILLUSTRATION 6-22   BACKGROUND SHAPE ANALYSIS OF "HANDBALL"**

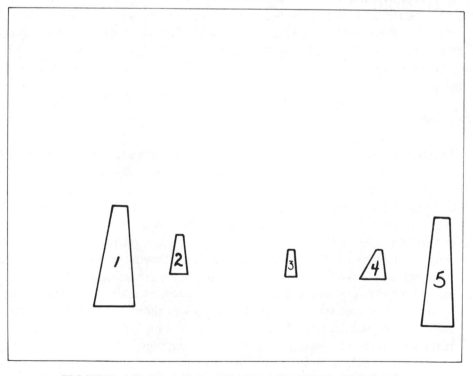

**ILLUSTRATION 6-23A   SHAPE ANALYSIS OF PEOPLE**

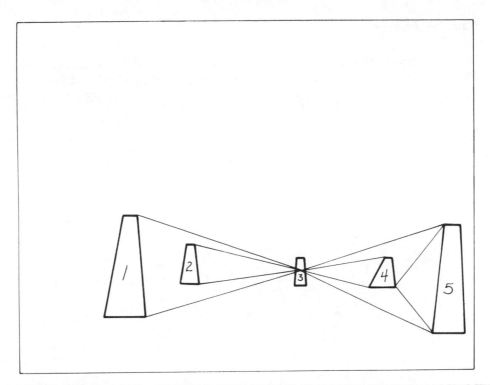

**ILLUSTRATION 6-23B   SPATIAL TRIANGLES CREATED BY EYE MOVEMENT**

of rectangle 1. Have children identify and draw other spatial triangles in different colors on the drawing of Illustration 6-23A.

- Display the print of Ben Shahn's *Handball* beside the two drawings. Have children observe that the boys in the print are the rectangles in the drawing of Illustration 6-23A. The building scape in the print is represented by the rectangles in the drawing of Illustration 6-22. When the drawing of Illustration 6-22 is combined with the drawing of Illustration 6-23A as evident in the print, the spatial triangles are still very visible. On the drawing of Illustration 6-23A, cover with a piece of paper rectangle 3 that represents the boy pitching. Have children notice how the composition suddenly has no meaning. Explain that the artist evidently had a reason for every shape he placed within the composition.
- Display Grant Wood's *Fall Plowing* and Van Gogh's *Cafe De Nuit*. Have children select one of the two prints to analyze, that is, to find the obvious and spatial shapes.
- From the gray, black, and white construction paper, cut the obvious and spatial shapes appearing in the print selected for analysis.
- On the bogus paper, arrange and paste the shapes to approximate the composition of the analyzed print.
- Paint a thin line of paste around the edges of a shape.
- Put yarn on top of the paste and press into position so that it outlines the shape.
- Continue this process until each shape is outlined with yarn. *Note:* Two or three colors of yarn may be used to form a double or triple yarn outline around some shapes.

### Can You Imagine . . .

Do the complete shape analysis on burlap with chalk and fill in the areas with yarn.
Make the shapes on white drawing paper with one or more colored felt markers.
Do a shape analysis of Maurice Utrillo's *Sacre Coeur* or Van Gogh's *The Steel Bridge*.

# CHAPTER 7

# CREATIVE LETTERING FROM SHAPES

Here is an opportunity to free the child from thinking of lettering as being a conventional block form, even in size and solid in color. Lettering is an individual and personal experience in creativity. The lettering of a message should be and is an integral part of the thought being portrayed. Size, color, shape, and placement of the word or words are of equal importance and must be considered simultaneously when planning a composition involving letters or lettering.

## BEFORE YOU BEGIN

Show samples of words from magazines, circulars, book covers, etc., that use some of the same letters. Point to and name one of the letters. Ask the children to describe the way the letter looks in each of the samples in which it is used. Encourage the use of adjectives such as *tall, short, fat, thin, wide, narrow*.

Provide children with 9″ × 12″ manila paper for this experiment:

Cut an irregular shape from the paper. (See Figure 7-1A.)

Cut away small parts of the shape to make the letter **R** (Figure 7-1B) without changing the basic shape of the paper. Remember the original shape of the paper must be noticeable in the shape of the **R**.

Cut a different irregular shape and make the letter **R** again (See Figure 7-2.)

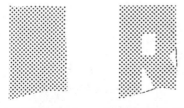

**FIGURE 7-1A    FIGURE 7-1B**
**SHAPING A**
**LETTER**

**FIGURE 7-2**
**ALTERNATE**
**SHAPE**

Cut more irregular shapes and experiment with forming capital and small letters.

A little practice with this basic technique will enable children to begin with the following self-image building activities that motivate creative lettering.

## NAMES IN SPACE (GRADES K-2)

To complete a composition of cutout magazine pictures by filling the spaces between the pictures with creative lettering.

*You'll Need . . .*

Scissors • magazines • pastel construction paper 9″ × 12″ (1 color per child's choice) • paste • paste dabbers or brushes • crayons • name models (optional) • cardboard scraps • small empty jars (or similar containers for paint) • mixtures of orange and white tempera paint, and yellow and white tempera paint.

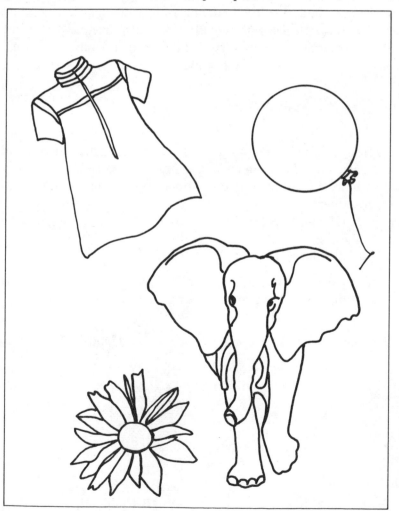

**ILLUSTRATION 7-1A**
**NAMES IN SPACE**

**ILLUSTRATION 7-1B**

*Procedures . . .*

- Have the children cut out magazine pictures of five small objects (flower, ball, animal, can of food, dress, tree, etc.) all the same color. *Note:* Children may select their colors or you may designate certain colors if you wish to reinforce color recognition. It is not necessary for the younger children to cut on the line.
- Choose a pastel color of construction paper.
- Paste the magazine pictures in any positions on the paper so that they do not touch each other as shown in Illustration 7-1A.
- With crayon, have children write their names in the spaces between and around their pictures (Illustration 7-1B). *Note:* For those children who can not write their names independently, give them name models from which to copy. Assure them that, to write their names in the spaces, they can make the letters go up, down, around, sideways, etc. First names or first and last names may be used.
- Have children dip the cardboard scraps in the tempera paint and brush color lightly

onto the tiny areas that do not contain letters or pictures. *Note:* Children may use either mixture or both mixtures of tempera paint.

### *Can You Imagine . . .*

Stack several oatmeal boxes and glue each to the other. Wrap the structure with brown kraft paper and tape securely. To complete this totem pole, each child prints his name with crayon or a felt marker so that the pole is covered with names. Use as a table decoration.

Use the procedures for "Names in Space" to cover large packing boxes. Use these as individual library tables in a corner of the room.

From the "Names in Space" composition, cut a portion that includes the child's name and at least a part of the magazine picture. With tape attach this cutout portion above or below a hook in the coat room.

## FROM INITIALS TO PENDANTS (GRADES 3-4)

To form letters creatively from a preselected shape.

### *You'll Need . . .*

Scissors ● manila paper 9″ × 12″ ● colored construction paper 9″ × 12″ (1 color per child's choice) ● pencils ● lightweight cardboard 9″ × 12″ or shirt boards ● scrap paper ● paste ● paste dabbers or brushes ● 1 pair of punchers ● 2′ lengths of string or yarn.

### *Procedures . . .*

- Have children free cut a circle, a square, and a triangle (each approximately 3″ in size) from the manila paper. *Note:* The shapes need not be perfect in form.
- Choose a color of construction paper.
- On the construction paper and on the cardboard, have children trace with a pencil around each of the manila paper shapes.
- Cut out the cardboard and the construction paper shapes.
- Cut the manila circle into two parts and fit the parts together again so that the cut edges are in vertical position.
- On scrap paper have children write their initials, first and last.
- Study the first initial and then cut it from the left part of the circle (Illustration 7-2A) so that the basic shape of the half circle remains. *Note:* Demonstrate with your initial if necessary. Also, have extra manila paper available so that children who may not like their first attempted letters can try again.
- Cut the last initial (Illustration 7-2B) from the other part of the circle.
- Trace around both initials on the construction paper circle and cut them out. *Note:* Have children fit the initials on the circle first to observe the fit of the letters within the plane of the shape.

**ILLUSTRATION 7-2A**                              **ILLUSTRATION 7-2B**

**INITIALS FROM CURVED SHAPES**

- Paste the construction paper letters on the cardboard circle.
- Punch a hole in the top of the initialed cardboard circle.
- Thread the string through the hole and tie a knot in the string where the outer edge of the circle above the hole touches the string. (See Illustration 7-3.)
- Repeat these procedures with the same initials using the triangle (Illustration 7-4) and square (Illustration 7-5). *Note:* The children may choose their favorite pendant to wear on different days.

**ILLUSTRATION 7-3**
**CIRCLE PENDANT**

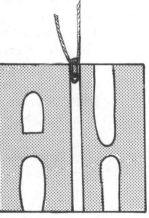

**ILLUSTRATION 7-5**
**SQUARE PENDANT**

**ILLUSTRATION 7-4   TRIANGLE PENDANT**

*Can You Imagine . . .*

Use the pendants for bookmarks.

Make pendants from initials cut from thin cork and mount on geometric shapes cut from cork.

Use a friend's initials to make a pendant, or plan exchange of pendants on Valentine's Day.

## PIN YOUR NAME (GRADES 5-6)

To create a composition from individually shaped letters.

*You'll Need . . .*

Scissors • manila paper 9″ × 12″ • pencils • colored construction paper 9″ × 12″ • paste • paste dabbers or brushes • lightweight cardboard 9″ × 12″ • safety pins • transparent tape.

*Procedures . . .*

- Have children cut several of each of these shapes (about 1″) from manila paper: circles, squares, and triangles.
- Have children select as many shapes from the cut shapes as needed in order to have a shape for each letter of their first or last names. *Note:* The children may choose all of one shape, or select a combination of two or more different shapes. More shapes can be cut if necessary.
- Cut the letters of the name from the shapes. (See Illustration 7-6A.) *Note:* Encourage children to cut as little as possible so that each letter will look like the original shape of the paper.
- Trace around these letters with a pencil on the construction paper and cut them out.
- Paste the letters on the cardboard and cut them out again.
- Have children spell their names on their desks, arranging the letters so that each letter is involved with another in overlapping positions as suggested in Illustration 7-6B. *Note:* Remind children that, even though there is overlapping, each letter must be identifiable.

**ILLUSTRATION 7-6A   NAME PIN**

**ILLUSTRATION 7-6B**

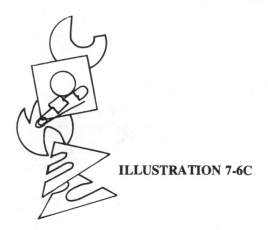

**ILLUSTRATION 7-6C**

- Paste the letters together in the desired arrangement.
- Turn the joined letters over and secure a safety pin (Illustration 7-6C) to the back of the name with two layers of transparent tape.

*Can You Imagine . . .*

Cover small shopping bags with a continuous design of cutout letters pasted in overlapping positions.

Cut out letters of the first name from cork. Paste the letters in overlapping positions. Make a key ring by punching a hole in one end of the name and inserting a notebook ring.

Follow the procedures for "Pin Your Name" but do not add a safety pin. Use the name as a signature model and copy it on work papers.

## LETTERED MULTI-PURPOSE BOXES (GRADES K-2)

To use creative lettering in a functional design.

*You'll Need . . .*

Newspaper want ad sections • paste • paste dabbers or brushes • shoe boxes (1 per group of 3 children) • scissors • magazines • newspaper • waxed paper • shellac • 3 paintbrushes • turpentine • an empty jar • two paper towels.

*Procedures . . .*

- Have children, working in groups of three, tear newspaper want ad sections into circular, square and triangular shapes.
- Paste the shapes in overlapping position on the sides, bottom, and lid of the shoe box. *Note:* Remind children to cover corners (Illustration 7-7A) as well as sides and bottom.
- Write a different letter on the board for each group. *Note:* For example, write **m** for one group, **p** for another, **a** for a third group, and so on.

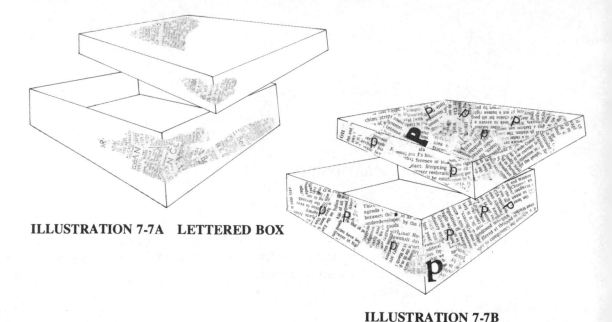

**ILLUSTRATION 7-7A   LETTERED BOX**

**ILLUSTRATION 7-7B**

- Have the groups each cut a variety of examples of their designated letter from the magazines. *Note:* Encourage them to look for tall, short, fat, and thin examples of various styles. Explain that they may want to leave a little of the magazine paper surrounding the letter.
- Paste the cutout letters on the sides of the newspaper covered box (Illustration 7-7B).
- Cover a table with a layer of newspaper and a layer of waxed paper, and place the box and shellac on top.
- Have the groups take turns shellacking their boxes and lids. *Note:* Shellac the bottom of the box last. Place the boxes "bottoms up" and lids right side up on waxed paper to dry. To clean the brushes, put them in the empty jar and add enough turpentine to cover the bristles. Swish the brushes around in the liquid until all paint is dissolved from the bristles. Place brushes on the paper towels to dry.

*Can You Imagine . . .*

Write a common word like *and, the, of, for, you, to,* or *that* on the board for each group. They cut a variety of examples of their word from the magazines and paste on the newspaper covered boxes.

Make different samples of letter cutouts from various kinds of paper and cloth. Cut letters from magazines, too. Store the letters in the multi-purpose boxes. Children help choose letters from the collection to form titles and labels for classroom displays.

Cut sponges into rectangular pieces of different sizes and place them in the newspaper covered boxes. During a free choice period, children form letters by positioning the pieces together and securing them with white glue.

## ACTION PICTURES (GRADES 3-4)

To create a feeling of action with lettering, magazine pictures and composition.

*You'll Need . . .*

Magazine and newspaper pictures of people in action poses ● scissors ● manila paper 6″ × 9″ (4 sheets per child) ● brown kraft paper 24″ × 10″ ● bogus paper 20″ × 15″ ● crayons.

*Procedures . . .*

- Display the magazine and newspaper pictures. Ask children to describe the action in each picture. Point to and discuss positions of body parts (especially head, neck, shoulders, torso, foot, arm) of the pictured people.
- Have individual children demonstrate other actions involving large muscles: reaching, twisting, stretching, leaning, etc. Point out positions of the child's body.
- Free cut from a sheet of manila paper a figure in an action pose that was pictured or demonstrated. *Note:* Children may cut figures from the other pieces of manila paper until they have at least one form that they feel shows action.
- Have children think of a word that best indicates the action of the figure.
- From the brown kraft paper, cut a large shape, not to exceed 5″ in any direction.
- Cut the shape into as many pieces as there are letters in the selected action word (Illustration 7-8A) and fit the pieces back together again.
- Cut away portions of the kraft pieces beginning with the first piece on the left, to form the letters of the word. (See Illustration 7-8B.) *Note:* Remind children to cut away only the paper necessary to form the letter and yet keep the basic shape of the piece of paper.

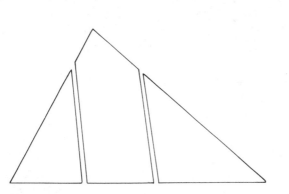
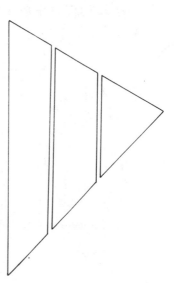

**ILLUSTRATION 7-8A   LETTERING OF ACTION WORD**

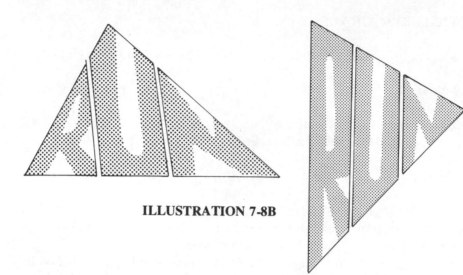

**ILLUSTRATION 7-8B**

- On the bogus paper have children experiment with arrangements of the action figure and the word. *Note:* Suggest ways of overlapping figure and word (Illustration 7-9).

**ILLUSTRATION 7-9**

**WAYS OF OVERLAPPING**

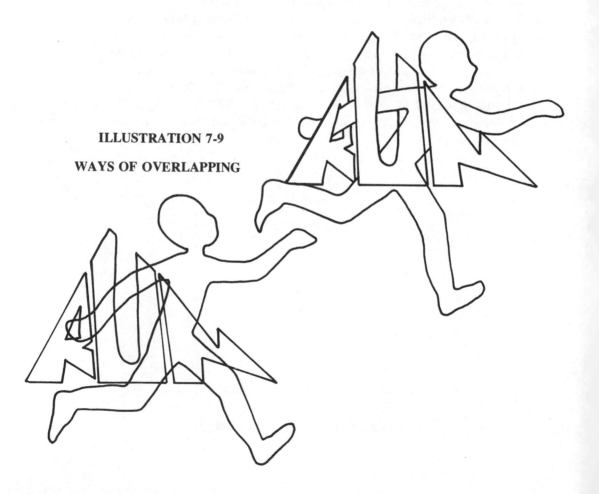

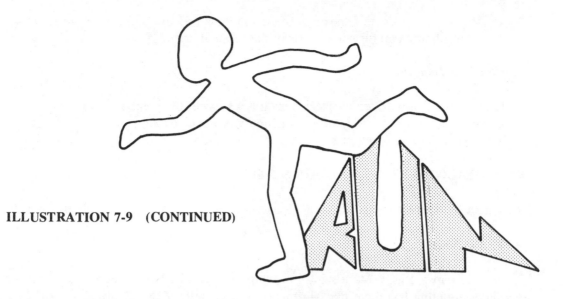

**ILLUSTRATION 7-9   (CONTINUED)**

- Trace with a thin crayon line around the arrangement.
- Repeat the tracing steps by overlapping the figure and word until the bogus paper is filled with an interesting grouping of traced shapes. (See Illustration 7-10.)

**ILLUSTRATION 7-10   TRACED SHAPE REPETITION**

- Apply a heavy coat of one color of crayon on the figures and a different color on the letters, being careful not to destroy the original crayon lines.

*Can You Imagine . . .*

Create an "Action Corner" by covering a wall with the compositions.
Create a composition using only an action word and several synonyms.
With water color, paint over the crayon composition.

## SEE-THROUGH LETTERS (GRADES 5-6)

To create a transparent composition by repeating a letter, varying its size, shape, and style.

*You'll Need . . .*

Manila paper 18″ × 24″ • scissors • various colors of tissue paper • straight pins • reversible mounting board cut into various sized rectangles 9″ × 12″ to 12″ × 14″ or shirt board • one part glue and two parts water solution • paintbrushes • empty jars or similar containers for holding solution.

*Procedures . . .*

- Have children each select a letter of the alphabet and from the manila paper free cut as many variations of the letter as possible. *Note:* Encourage cutting capital and lowercase forms of different sizes, widths, heights, shapes, etc. (See Illustration 7-11).

**ILLUSTRATION 7-11   FREE CUT LETTER VARIATIONS**

- Choose at least three colors of tissue paper and stack the sheets.
- Pin the manila letters to the three layers of tissue and cut around the letters.
- Unpin the tissue letters and arrange them in overlapping positions on the mounting board as shown in Illustration 7-12. *Note:* Encourage children to experiment with spacing by creating open areas of various sizes as letters are added. The composition of letters should extend over the entire surface of the mounting board, with some letters touching the edges of the board. Different colors will be formed as colors overlap colors.
- Paint over the tissue letters and the entire surface of the mounting board with the glue and water solution. *Note:* Remind children to keep the brush wet with the solution; a dry brush will pull the tissue off the mounting board. After the composition dries, put weight (books, magazines, etc.) on the boards to prevent curling.

**ILLUSTRATION 7-12**

**LETTER SHAPES
OVERLAPPING**

*Can You Imagine . . .*

Repeat the procedures for ''See-Through Letters,'' using 8½" × 11" mounting board. When dry, cut in half lengthwise. Cut blank manila or writing paper the same size. For an attractive scratch pad, punch holes in one end of the paper and the two pieces of board. Place the writing paper between the pieces of mounting board and bind with yarn.

Add a bit of texture to one or two letters in the arrangement. On felt or other fabric, pin the manila patterns of the letters selected. Cut around patterns and glue resulting cloth letters over matching tissue ones.

Make "See-Through Numerals."

## HELPFUL REMINDER POSTERS (GRADES K-2)

To combine lettering with drawings.

*You'll Need . . .*

Colored construction paper 12″ × 18″ • crayons • magazines • scissors • paste • paste dabbers or brushes.

*Procedures . . .*

- Have children dictate rules and helpful reminders that will enable the school and classroom to be a better place for all. Encourage them to keep the rules short, for example: "Make a New Friend," "Pick Up Trash," "Walk Down Stairs." Write the rules in three lists: one list written in all capital letters, another list of the same

**ILLUSTRATION 7-13A**     **ILLUSTRATION 7-13B**

**POSTER FROM CRAYON AND CUT LETTERS**

rules but written in uppercase and lowercase letters, and the third list with the same rules written in all lowercase letters.

- Have children each select a rule and illustrate it with crayons on construction paper of the color of their choice. (See Illustration 7-13A.)
- From magazines cut words and/or letters to form words that appear in the rule selected. *Note:* The models on the board of the different printed forms of the rules will help the younger children feel comfortable in using either lowercase letters, capitals or both. Kindergarteners may need help in finding words and letters. Encourage them to compare words and letters on the board with the ones in the magazines in order to have the exact word needed.
- Experiment with arranging words and/or letters to form the rule on the paper containing the illustration. *Note:* Gear a discussion of "Poster Musts" (see below) to the maturity of the children. Demonstrate with commercial posters if necessary.
- Paste the words and/or letters in place. (See Illustration 7-13B.)

*Can You Imagine . . .*

Use an 18″ circle shape instead of the 12″ × 18″ paper.
Paste bits of cloth and yarn on the crayon illustration.
Use wood scraps, crumpled paper, and other real objects to illustrate the rules. Then paste on the words cut from magazines or from newspapers.

## A ROUND POSTER (GRADES 3-4)

To experiment with design and lettering on a three-dimensional surface.

*You'll Need . . .*

Three or four commercial posters • manila paper 18″ × 24″ • paste • paste dabbers or brushes • masking or transparent tape • newspaper want ad sections • pencils • scrap paper • scissors • magazines • 1 pair of punchers • yarn.

*Procedures . . .*

- Use the commercial posters to illustrate and discuss the following "Poster Musts": colors must relate to the subject (see Chapters 1-3); words must relate in size and color to the importance they play in the message; message must be brief, meaningful, and easy to read; leftover space must form a part of the overall composition of the poster; illustration, if any, must be free of cluttering details, must appeal to the viewer, and emphasize the message.
- Have the children roll the manila paper to form a cylinder that is about 7″ in diameter and 18″ long. *Note:* The 18″ × 24″ paper rolled to this diameter results in a strong, durable cylinder.
- Secure the cylinder with paste or tape.

- Paste cut up or torn pieces of the newspaper want ad sections on the cylinder, covering it completely.
- Have children write on the scrap paper a message that they would like to put on their cylinders. *Note:* To encourage them to think of different messages, suggest a few ideas such as "Have brains—will learn." "Happiness is being cool." "Share your smile."
- Cut out words and/or letters from magazines to form the message and assemble these in order on the desk. (See Illustration 7-14.) *Note:* Have children consider methods

**share YOUR Smile.**

**ILLUSTRATION 7-14**

**CUT OUT LETTERING FOR POSTER**

of arranging words on the cylindrical form as shown in Illustration 7-15. Demonstrate these methods by holding a cylinder in one hand and dramatizing with the other hand how messages might be arranged. At the same time use descriptive words like winding, stair step, stacking, spiralling, etc.

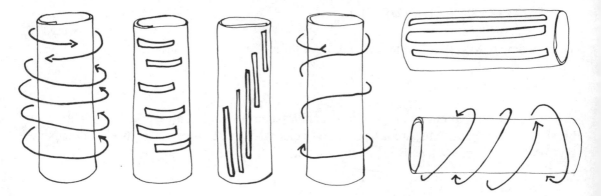

**ILLUSTRATION 7-15   SUGGESTED LETTER ARRANGEMENTS**

- Paste the words and/or letters on the cylinder in the desired arrangement.
- For vertical posters (Illustration 7-16), punch two holes opposite each other, about 1″ from the top of one end; for horizontal posters (Illustration 7-17) punch one hole in each end.
- Thread yarn through these holes and form a loop by tying the ends. (See Illustrations 7-16 and 7-17.)
- Add a tassel of yarn to the vertical poster (Illustration 7-16); yarn fringe or stripes may be pasted on each end of the horizontal poster (Illustration 7-17).

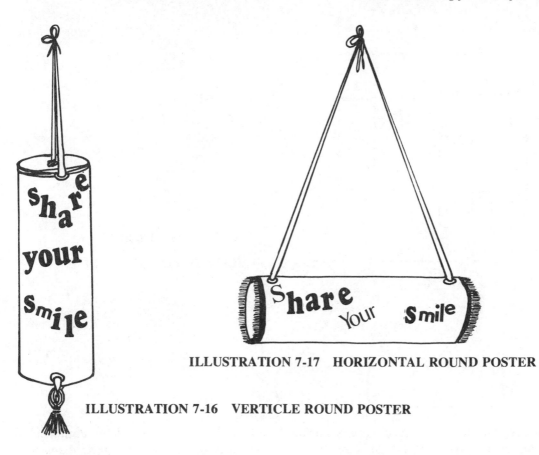

**ILLUSTRATION 7-17   HORIZONTAL ROUND POSTER**

**ILLUSTRATION 7-16   VERTICLE ROUND POSTER**

*Can You Imagine . . .*

On a cylinder of white construction paper, use black lettering and a black tassel.

Create a poster mobile. Suspend several posters by string from a mobile frame that is made of two or more wire bars joined by different lengths of string. Suspend from a single bar. (See Illustration 7-18.)

Create a stabile. Punch holes at each end of a cylinder. Insert heavy twine through holes at one end and tie for hanging. Attach a piece of twine in the same manner at the other end. Join one cylinder to another cylinder by tying the ends of the twine together creating a chain of cylinders. Attach loose twine ends overhead and attach opposite ends to the floor.

## PICTURELESS POSTERS (GRADES 5-6)

To use creative lettering as the total composition with emphasis on the importance of color, size, and shape of lettering.

*You'll Need . . .*

Manila paper 9″ × 12″ • pencils • cloth scraps • colored construction paper scraps •

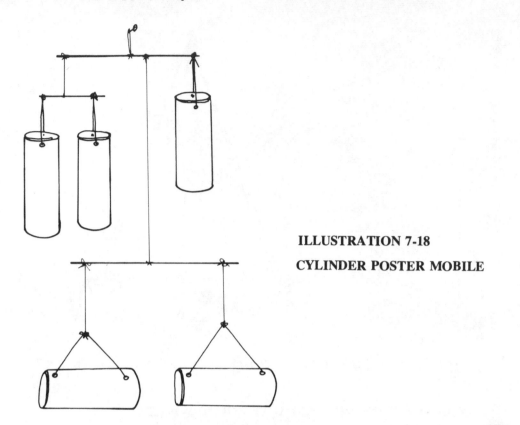

**ILLUSTRATION 7-18**

**CYLINDER POSTER MOBILE**

newspaper want ad sections • scissors • poster board 18″ × 24″ or reversible mounting board or construction paper 18″ × 24″ • rubber cement or paste or white glue • paste dabbers or brushes.

*Procedures . . .*

- Print the following open-end statements on the chalkboard:

| | |
|---|---|
| Happiness is_____. | Politeness is_____. |
| Love is_____. | Spring is_____. |
| Autumn is_____. | A season is _____. |
| Summer is_____. | A friend is_____. |
| Winter is_____. | Kindness is_____. |

These subjects present children with the challenge of completing the sentences with their own meaningful words.
- On the manila paper, have the children copy the sentences and complete each one. Study the completed sentences and select one to be made into a poster.
- On the reverse side of the manila paper, experiment with different ways of writing or printing the sentence to emphasize meaning. *Note:* Encourage children to consider which word is the most important. Explain that the size of a word can help express the meaning of the message. (See Illustrations 7-19 and 7-20.)
- Select scrap materials and newspaper want ad sections to use for lettering. *Note:*

**ILLUSTRATION 7-19**         **ILLUSTRATION 7-20**

**LETTERING SIZE ESTABLISHES MEANING**

Explain that different materials may be needed for different words in the sentence. Ask children to think about the color a word may suggest.

- Cut irregular shapes from the selected scrap materials (Illustration 7-21A) for the words. *Note:* Emphasize that each word should relate to the whole message through color, size, shape, and material so that the viewer becomes emotionally involved and immediately grasps the intended message.
- Cut the materials into as many parts as there are letters in the words. (See Illustration 7-21B.)
- Cut letters from the pieces of material (Illustration 7-21C).
- On the poster board, experiment with several arrangements of the words. *Note:* Suggest the following as children do this procedure: words need not be centered on the poster (Illustration 7-22); words may be angled (Illustration 7-23); portions of words may overlap (Illustration 7-24); an imaginary border should surround the composition.
- Paste the desired arrangement on the poster board.

*Can You Imagine . . .*

Create a ''long'' poster by arranging a message on a 9″ × 24″ strip of construction paper.

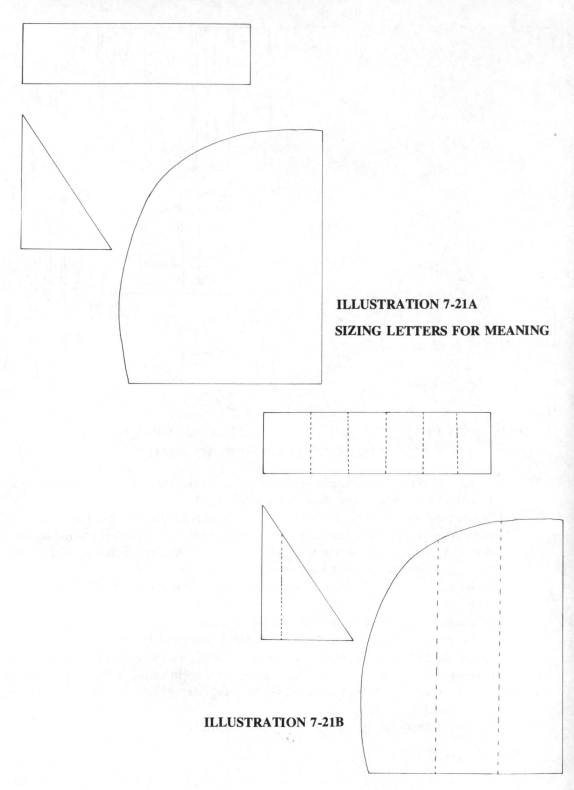

**ILLUSTRATION 7-21A**

**SIZING LETTERS FOR MEANING**

**ILLUSTRATION 7-21B**

**ILLUSTRATION 7-21C**

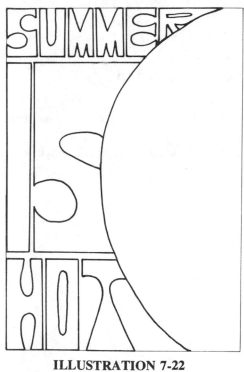

**ILLUSTRATION 7-22**

**OFF CENTER ARRANGEMENT**

**ILLUSTRATION 7-23**

**ANGLED WORDS**

**ILLUSTRATION 7-24   OVERLAPPING WORDS**

Cut the lettering from thin pieces of cork shapes. Arrange and glue the letters on poster board.

Use printed wallpaper for the lettering and mount the message on black construction paper.

# CHAPTER 8

# MIXING MEDIA

In previous chapters different media have been combined in the culmination of some projects. However, the mixing of media has not been the primary emphasis. This chapter provides that special stress on combining two or more media to achieve a variety of compositional effects. The projects are designed to encourage children to contemplate independently how a medium will work with other media and to experiment with them to achieve different or unusual effects.

## BEFORE YOU BEGIN

Take a trip to the art museum to see compositions that are done in more than one medium such as water color and ink, cloth and paint, pastels and ink or charcoal, and water color and other media. Look for many different compositional effects achieved by combining media.

Display some of the following reproductions of mixed media compositions. Call attention to the media used in each.

Homer's *Skating in Central Park* (ink and water color), *The Wrecked Schooner* (water color and charcoal).

Audubon's *Black-Tailed Hare* (pencilled drawing, ink, water color, and chalk).

Whistler's *The Doorway, Venice* (pastel and charcoal).

Saura's *Figure* (cardboard, paint, torn paper, and ink).

Burri's *Composition Red and White* (cloth, wallpaper, and plaster).

One of the most familiar methods of mixing media is the crayon resist, brushing water base paint such as water color or tempera over crayoned drawings. The oil or wax in the crayon resists the paint while other areas without crayon accept it. Try the following crayon resist; apply the crayons heavily.

*For kindergarten through the second grade:* have children pretend that 9″ drawing paper circles are very warm. They use three bright colors of crayons to color it so that the colors seem to melt and run into each other.

*For third and fourth grades:* children draw numerals on 9″ drawing paper circles with three colors of crayons. The numerals may vary in size and thickness, but they must overlap. Children turn the circle in different positions as they draw the numerals.

*For fifth and sixth grades:* children think of a season and of words that remind them of that season. They write the season name and the words in three colors of crayon on 9″ drawing paper circles, using cursive or manuscript lettering. Encourage them to write legibly and to turn the circle a little after writing a word. Words may be of different sizes.

Spread newspaper on a table. Put six cakes of black water color on paper towels on the table. Place six paintbrushes and six paint cups of water (half-filled) on the table. After children (kindergarten through sixth graders) complete their circular compositions, they take turns painting over the crayon with the black water color. Remind them to dip the brush in the water, dab the brush on the water color cake, and then brush the color on the paper. (See Figures 8-1, 8-2, 8-3.) Place the compositions on newspaper to dry.

FIGURE 8-1          FIGURE 8-2          FIGURE 8-3

Make a wall border of the circles on a white background.

Have children look for other examples of mixed media in magazines and books. Make a display of examples brought in by the children.

## THE BODY NATURALLY (GRADES K-2)

To do a figure drawing.

*You'll Need . . .*

Three or more of these prints: Renoir's *Girl with Watering Can*, Manet's *The Fifer*, Degas' *Dancer Bowing with Bouquet*, Gainsborough's *Blue Boy*, Toulouse-Lautrec's *At the Moulin Rouge: The Dance,* Murillo's *The Young Beggar* • scissors • picture magazines (1 per child) • paste • paste dabbers or brushes • pastel colors of construction paper 9″ × 12″ • crayons.

*Procedures* . . .

- Display the prints. Ask children to look at the details of the clothing (collars, buttons, color, pattern, etc.). Next, consider what the figure is doing (standing, holding something, bowing, etc.). Explain that the background of these compositions is the space behind the people. Ask them to compare the backgrounds and describe what each contains (color, objects, and people).
- Have children carefully cut out a magazine picture of a head (with neck) of a person (no smaller than 1″ in one dimension and not to exceed 2″ in the other direction).
- Have children paste the magazine cutout on the construction paper near the top. (See Illustration 8-1A.)
- Draw a crayon body and some clothes on the construction paper to go with the magazine head. (See Illustration 8-1B.)
- On the clothing, add crayon details like patterns, buttons, pockets, etc., and color the clothes. *Note:* Apply crayon heavily.
- Blend three colors of crayon in the background around the figure. *Note:* Children may put trees and houses in the background.

**ILLUSTRATION 8-1A**                **ILLUSTRATION 8-1B**

**CREATING A FULL FIGURE**

*Can You Imagine . . .*

Cut out the completed figure. Arrange a border of the children's figures. Cut houses and other city signs from magazines and use them behind the figures to create an urban setting.

On a 6″ × 12″ cardboard strip, draw vertical lines to resemble a length of fence. Paste the cutout figure on the fence. (See Illustration 8-2.) Join the fences together in zigzag fashion. Stand them on the window ledges or book shelves.

Cut from a magazine the torso of a person. Paste the picture on the construction paper. Complete the person by drawing crayon head, legs, arms, etc. Add crayon background items.

**ILLUSTRATION 8-2  STANDING FIGURE**

## TRANSPARENT AND OPAQUE SHAPES (GRADES 3-4)

To assemble a composition of overlapping transparent and opaque shapes.

*You'll Need . . .*

Print of Feininger's *The Church* • pictures and photographs of various types of buildings • newspaper • assorted colors of square and rectangular pieces of tissue paper not to exceed 3″ in any direction (about 30 per child's choice of 4 colors) • white construction paper 9″ × 12″ • No. 12 paintbrushes • 3 parts water and 1 part glue solution (1/3 cup per child) • water cups • scissors • felt and other cloth pieces not to exceed 2″ in any direction (about 6 per child's choice).

## *Procedures* . . .

- Have children examine the print by Feininger. Call attention to the many rectangles created by the overlapping colors. Explain that many of the shapes are created by transparent color, that is, color showing through color.
- Display the pictures of the buildings. Compare the basic shapes of the total structures, the rooftops, the windows and doors, additions to the basic structures (columns, balconies, wings, etc.). Ask which buildings appear as two or more sections joined together.
- Cover the desks with newspaper.
- Have children place one piece of tissue paper on the construction paper.
- Place another piece of tissue paper so that it overlaps the first piece. (See Illustration 8-3A.) *Note:* Explain that these overlapping tissue pieces create building shapes.
- Paint over the surface of the two pieces of tissue paper with the water and glue solution. *Note:* Children should moisten the brush thoroughly with the solution. Cover the edges of the tissue with the solution.
- Cut small door and window shapes from the cloth pieces and glue them on the tissue building shapes.
- Arrange and glue on more building shapes, adding windows and doors (Illustration 8-3B). *Note:* Shapes must overlap. Encourage children to use the pictures of buildings as reference. Remind them to brush the solution over all tissue shapes added.
- Glue on one color of tissue shapes for the sky.
- Cover the ground area with some of the remaining tissue scraps.

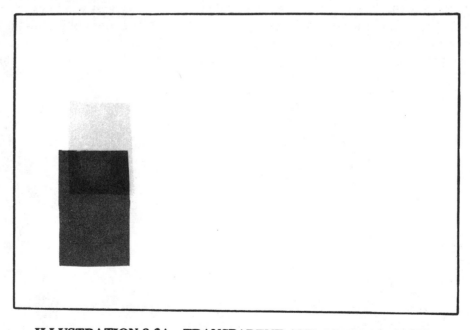

**ILLUSTRATION 8-3A   TRANSPARENT AND OPAQUE SHAPES**

**ILLUSTRATION 8-3B**

*Can You Imagine . . .*

Paste tiny black tissue strips on the building shapes to suggest windows and details.

Create a composition of building shapes using two values of one color of tissue on white construction paper. (See Chapter 3 on values.)

Arrange the tissue and cloth pieces to create a single, elongated building shape on a

**ILLUSTRATION 8-4   BUILDING COMPOSITION**

6″ × 1?″ construction paper strip. After the composition dries, paste yellow construction paper rectangles on the building to represent lighted windows and doors. (See Illustration 8-4.)

## FIGURES ON PRINT (GRADES 5-6)

To create a composition of continuous line figure drawings.

*You'll Need . . .*

Three or 4 of these prints: Bellows' *Dempsey and Firpo*, Homer's *Snap the Whip*, Degas' *Miss Cassatt at the Louvre*, Toulouse-Lautrec's *At the Moulin Rouge: The Dance*, Degas' *The Rehearsal* and *Rehearsal of a Ballet on the Stage*, Benton's *Cradling Wheat*, Bingham's *The Wood Boat,* and Mary Cassatt's *The Bath* • want ad newspaper page (4 sheets per child) • black felt markers • 2 or 3 instrumental recordings of songs of different tempos • record player or cassette player • crayons • paste • paste dabbers or brushes • white construction paper 12″ × 18″.

*Procedures . . .*

- Display the prints. List on the chalkboard verbs that children use to describe the action of the people in the prints. Discuss how each artist portrays people in action: Which persons seem stiff? Why? Which seem to be moving freely? Which person appears to have a relaxed stance? Why? Have children notice arm positions, tilt of head, shoulders, etc. Call attention to groupings of people and the overlapping of figures. Ask how the artist treats a figure to indicate depth in the composition. Which pictures appear to have all figures in the foreground?
- On one sheet of newspaper, have children draw with the felt marker a continuous line drawing of a figure similar to a gingerbread boy. (See Illustration 8-5.) *Note:* Encourage them to slightly drag the felt marker over the page, continuously extending the line in various directions, without lifting the marker until the drawing is completed.
- Have six children pose as models in the center of the room, facing in different directions with the rest of the class seated around them. *Note:* Encourage relaxed natural stances. Each pose assumed should be different. Remind models to stand still.
- Make on another sheet of newspaper continuous line drawings of one or two of the posed children. *Note:* Suggest the following to children as they proceed:
    - —Draw things as your eyes meet them. For example, you see the person's collar as you make the neck, so draw the collar at that time, too. (See Illustration 8-6.)
    - —Include all wrinkles, folds, pleats, buttons, etc., as you come to them. (See Illustration 8-7.)
    - —Change a line you are not satisfied with by simply drawing another one over it.
    - —Draw quickly while looking at the model and glancing occasionally at the

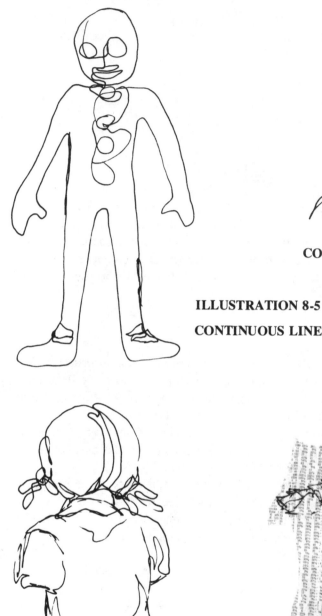

**ILLUSTRATION 8-6**

**CONTINUOUS LINE DRAWING OF HEAD**

**ILLUSTRATION 8-5**

**CONTINUOUS LINE DRAWING: GINGERBREAD BOY**

**ILLUSTRATION 8-8    FIGURE ON PRINT**

**ILLUSTRATION 8-7    CONTINUOUS LINE DRAWING WITH DETAILS**

paper. Try to establish a rhythm of looking from model to page while swinging the continuous line onto the paper. Use full-arm movement instead of just wrist action.

—Draw big.

*Note:* Models should hold poses 2 to 3 minutes only.

- Play a selection from one of the records for a second group of models to swing arms and twist torso in time to the music. *Note:* Encourage them to swing arms freely.
- Stop the music for the models to "freeze" in their positions and for children to quickly draw on another sheet of newspaper one of the poses. (See Illustration 8-8.) *Note:* Give these additional suggestions as children draw: When drawing the head, make only the shape of it and the shape of the hair. Do not draw facial features. Try to illustrate the motion that was just seen as you draw the model.
- Have another group of models perform "bend and stretch" movements and "freeze" in position for the class to make continuous line drawings on another sheet of the newspaper.
- Accent portions of the figures with two or three colors of crayons. *Note:* Remind children to avoid coloring over lines as they color portions of the figures.
- Tear around each continuous line drawing and paste one or more drawings on the white construction paper. *Note:* Excess newspaper surrounding the figures may overlap on the paper.

*Can You Imagine . . .*

Cut out the figures. Paste them on a crayon or water color landscape.

Cut out buildings from magazine pictures. Paste them in overlapping positions. Color in sky with crayon or water color. Cut out the continuous line figures and paste on this composition of buildings. (See Illustration 8-9.)

Construct a mural of the continuous line drawings. Children paint in the background with water colors or tempera paints. Use cardboard pieces for brushes.

## SEE HOW THEY BLOOM (GRADES K-2)

To combine shapes in a composition

*You'll Need . . .*

Picture collection of different kinds and colors of flowers • live flowers (optional) • a checkerboard • white construction paper 16″ × 16″ • paste • paste dabbers or brushes • colored construction paper 4″ × 4″ (8 per each child's choice) • crayons • scissors • different colored felt scraps about 3″ × 5″ (2 per child).

*Procedures . . .*

- Display the flower pictures on bulletin boards covered with white paper. Place the live flowers on a low table where children can examine them. Have children observe

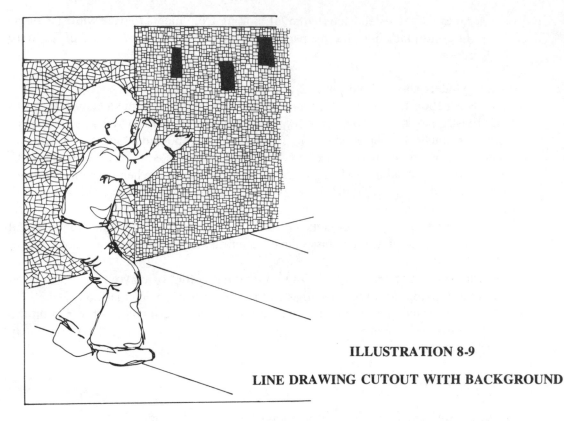

**ILLUSTRATION 8-9**

**LINE DRAWING CUTOUT WITH BACKGROUND**

and describe the shapes and colors of the blooms. Guide them in noting variations in the shapes.

- Show children the checkerboard and help them identify the arrangement of the two colors.
- Help children fold the white construction paper squares in half twice vertically and horizontally to create 16 small squares.
- Have children paste their eight colored squares in checkerboard fashion on the spaces of the folded construction paper. (See Illustration 8-10A.)
- Make bright crayon drawings of different flowers (Illustration 8-10B) in the white spaces.
- Cut small flower shapes from the felt and paste on the colored squares (Illustration 8-10C).

*Can You Imagine . . .*

Paint every other square on the folded construction paper with one color of tempera paint. Draw flowers in remaining white spaces with felt markers of various colors.

Paste a different color square on every other square on the folded construction paper. Paste cutout pictures of flowers in the white spaces. Draw black lines with a felt marker around the flowers.

Paint every other square on the folded construction paper with tempera. Cut out felt

ILLUSTRATION 8-10A                    ILLUSTRATION 8-10B

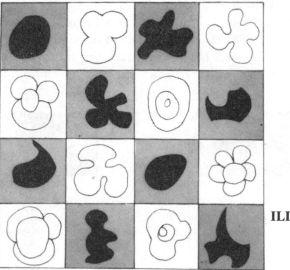

ILLUSTRATION 8-10C

**FLOWER AND GEOMETRIC SHAPES**

flowers and paste them in the white spaces. After the paint dries, paste cutout pictures of flowers on the painted squares.

## COLOR PATCHES WITH STILL LIFE (GRADES 3-4)

To create a composition with special emphasis on color effects.

*You'll Need . . .*

Prints of Van Gogh's *Sunflowers*, Degas' *Woman with Chrysanthemums*, Huysum's

*Still Life of Fruit*, Dufy's *Flowers*, Matisse's *Plum Blossoms*, *Green Background*, Redon's *Vase of Flowers*, Bonnard's *Bouquet de Fleurs* • crayons (24 colors per box) • manila paper 6" × 9" • scissors • fashion and picture magazines (1 per child) • paste • paste dabbers or brushes • shirt boards • magazine or catalog pictures of flower arrangements in a variety of containers • pencils • about 5 felt tip pens.

### Procedures . . .

- Show the prints. Explain the meaning of *still life* (a subject for a painting composed of inanimate objects). Have children discuss different ways artists interpret flower arrangements: Which flowers are the brightest? Which seem to look more realistic? Which flowers do you like most? Why? Which ones have the most details? Discuss colors used in the compositions.
- Have children color on the manila paper small patches of colors that best match the colors in a print they select.
- Cut from the magazines various sizes of rectangular colored patches that are values (See Chapter 3) of the crayon color patches.
- Arrange and paste these colored rectangles on the shirt board (Illustration 8-11A) so that three rectangles of empty space remain. *Note:* Each empty space should be a different size. The three spaces should be separated by color.
- Have children select one of the pictures or still life prints.
- In the *smallest rectangle* of space on the shirt board, draw lightly with pencil a small

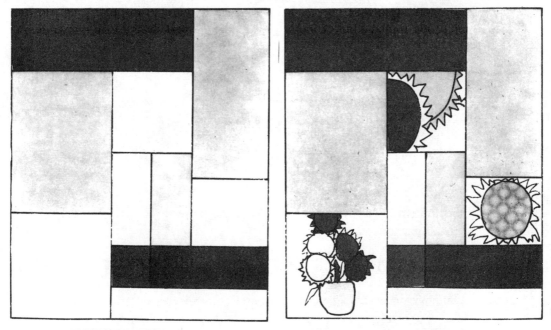

**ILLUSTRATION 8-11A**          **ILLUSTRATION 8-11B**

**COLOR PATCHES WITH STILL LIFE**

portion of the selected still life, for example, draw a bloom without stem or leaves. *Note:* Encourage children to fill that space with the drawing.

- In the *next smallest space* draw another small portion like a flower with leaves and part of stem, or more than one flower, or a small part of a group of flowers.
- In the *largest space* draw the whole still life arrangement. *Note:* Remind children to draw the container or vase last and to fill the space with the drawing.
- Color the three drawings with crayons that best match the colored rectangles pasted on the shirt board. *Note:* Color should not be put over the pencilled lines.
- Use felt tip pens to go over the pencilled lines of the drawing. (See Illustration 8-11B.)

### *Can You Imagine . . .*

Cut out magazine pictures of objects for a still life: food, glasses or bottles, or leaves. Make a still life arrangement of the pictures on the desk. Draw a different still life arrangement of these objects in each of the three spaces.

Cut out individual flowers from magazines. Arrange and paste a still life of cutout flowers in each of the three spaces. Draw a container for each and color with crayon.

Cut out three white construction paper rectangles that are the sizes of the empty spaces on the shirt board. Paint miniature water color still life on these shapes. Add accent lines of black crayon. Paste the miniatures in the spaces.

## WATER COLOR PLUS (GRADES 5-6)

To create a variety of effects in a still life composition.

### *You'll Need . . .*

Carton 4′ × 3′ × 2′ • cloth to drape over the carton • a potted leaf plant • 3 or 4 pieces of fruit • broken crayons with wrappings removed • white construction paper 9″ × 12″ • 1 bucket of water • paper towels (2 per child) • 12″ paintbrushes • water (1/2 cup per child) • paint cups • red, yellow, and blue water color cakes • black felt markers • empty bucket.

### *Procedures . . .*

- Set the carton upside down on a table. Cover the carton with the cloth. Arrange the plant and fruit on the cloth covered carton. Group the fruit and plant so that they overlap each other. Place the arrangement where all the children can see it without difficulty. *Note:* More than one arrangement like this may be placed around the room.
- Using the side of one piece of crayon, have children form on the construction paper shapes representing the plant and fruits. (See Illustration 8-12A.) *Note:* Encourage children to avoid drawing lines.
- Submerge the construction paper in the bucket of water and hold a paper towel under the paper to catch the water dripping.

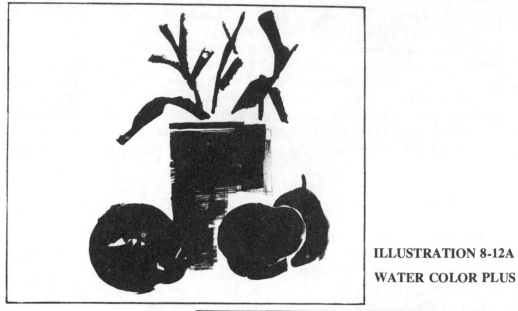

**ILLUSTRATION 8-12A**
**WATER COLOR PLUS**

**ILLUSTRATION 8-12B**

- Place the paper on the desk and smooth out the wrinkles. *Note:* This can be easily done by lifting the paper and placing it on the desk again, or brushing over the paper lightly with a brush filled with water.
- Wet the brush and then load it with water color and apply colors to various areas on the paper. *Note:* The water color should spread and blend, and some white spaces should be visible. These white spaces and the fuzzy areas of color enhance the composition.
- While the paper is wet, use the felt marker to draw lines to accent the still life shapes

(Illustration 8-12B). *Note:* Encourage children to avoid ''overworking'' the composition. Lines should be drawn lightly and quickly so that they add to the composition without dominating it. Pour water from the paint cups into the empty bucket. Dampen a paper towel in clean water and wipe off the cakes of paint.

*Can You Imagine* . . .

Paint rubber cement on some parts of the composition. Allow it to dry before wetting the paper. After adding the water color and the felt marker lines, let the composition dry. Gently rub the rubber cement to remove it, exposing the white paper.

Use several colors of crayon to form still life shapes. Then complete composition as directed in the project.

Wet the construction paper first. Then lightly sketch outlines of shapes to represent the still life with the felt marker. Brush water colors over the shapes. Allow the paper to dry before forming crayon shapes to accent the composition.

## CITY SHAPES (GRADES K-2)

To create a line and form impression.

*You'll Need* . . .

Prints of Marin's *Singer Building, Movement Fifth Avenue,* and *Lower Manhattan,* Hopper's *Seven A.M.* and *Sunday Morning,* Feininger's *The Church,* Hughie Lee Smith's *Boy on Roof* • 1 wallpaper sample book • scissors • paste • paste dabbers or brushes • pastel construction paper 12" × 18" • various colors of felt scraps (4 per child) • crayons.

*Procedures* . . .

- Show the prints. Help children identify the many and varied geometric shapes in the compositions. Look for squares, circles, triangles.
- Have children each choose a wallpaper page and cut it into 4 parts.
- Cut the wallpaper pieces into building shapes of different sizes.
- Paste the building shapes in overlapping position (Illustration 8-13A) on the construction paper.
- Have children each select four pieces of felt of different colors.
- Cut small window shapes from the felt and paste on the building shapes. (See Illustration 8-13B.)
- Paste on more building shapes formed from wallpaper and felt scraps. *Note:* Remind children to paste down all edges.
- Draw heavy, black crayon lines around each building and every window.
- Draw crayon sidewalks, make crayon bricks on some buildings, and add community items like telephone poles, stop lights, signs, etc. *Note:* Apply the crayon heavy. (See Illustration 8-13C.)
- Color the street and the sky with other colors.

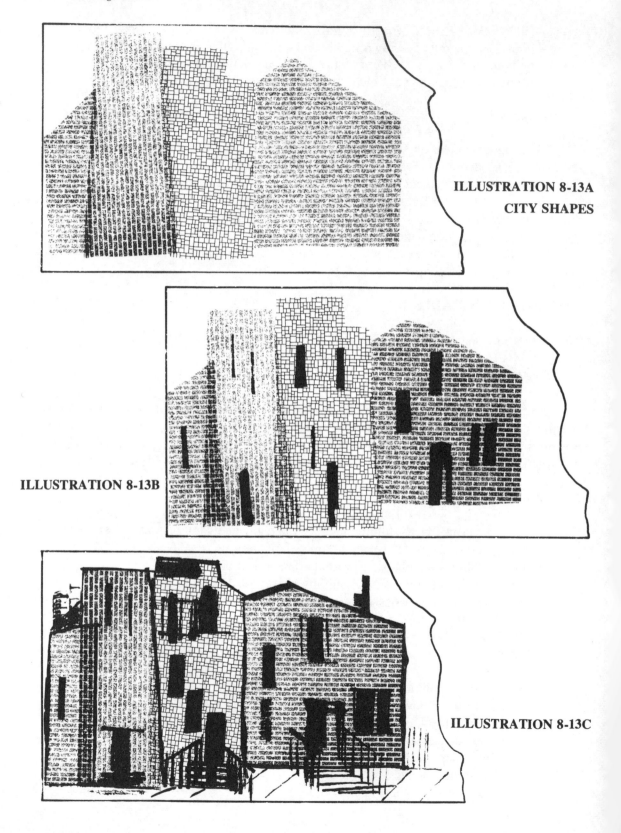

**ILLUSTRATION 8-13A
CITY SHAPES**

**ILLUSTRATION 8-13B**

**ILLUSTRATION 8-13C**

*Can You Imagine . . .*

Cut out shapes of trash cans, street signs, and lamp posts from construction paper. Paste them on the composition of shapes. Draw heavy black crayon lines around them.

Draw, color, and cut out people (and cats and dogs, too). Paste them on the sidewalks in the compositions.

Tape the compositions together to create a wall mural. Display the mural at the bottom of the wall. Children fashion people figures out of pipe cleaners and stand them in front of the mural.

## COMPOSITION OVER ONE (GRADES 3-4)

To combine a shape composition and a line composition to create a single statement.

*You'll Need . . .*

Photographs and magazine pictures of buildings • wallpaper sample book (1 page per child) • newspaper (1 page per child) • paste • paste dabbers or brushes • bogus paper 15" × 20" • manila paper 9" × 12" • crayons • black felt markers • colored chalk (2 colors per child's choice) • jar lids each containing about 1 tablespoon of water.

*Procedures . . .*

- Display the collection of photographs and pictures. Review the meaning of *silhouette*. Children compare the silhouettes of the buildings. Look for characteristics of architectural design that distinguish one silhouette from another (dome, steeple, chimney, basic shape, etc.).
- Have children tear out several building shapes from the wallpaper and newspaper pages. (See Illustration 8-14A.) *Note:* Encourage them to tear out some building shapes like ones they observed in the photographs and pictures.

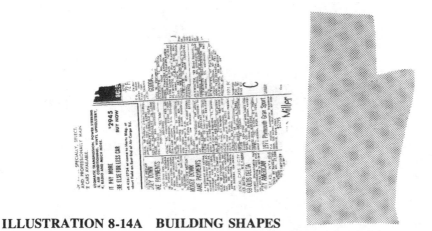

**ILLUSTRATION 8-14A   BUILDING SHAPES**

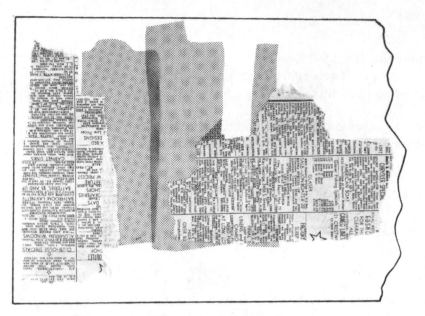

**ILLUSTRATION 8-14B**

- Experiment with different arrangements of the building silhouettes in overlapping positions.
- Paste the chosen arrangement of building shapes on the bogus paper. (See Illustration 8-14B.) *Note:* Have children put the composition aside and look at the photographs and pictures again.
- On the manila paper have children make a crayon continuous line drawing of one of the buildings in the collection. (See Illustration 8-15.) *Note:* Encourage children to avoid lifting the crayon, until the building is complete, to make a continuous line drawing. Remind them to hold the crayon loosely and to make a big building. They may try a second drawing on the back of the paper.

**ILLUSTRATION 8-15**

**SAMPLE CONTINUOUS LINE DRAWING**

**ILLUSTRATION 8-16**

**COMPOSITION OVER ONE**

- Do a series of crayon continuous line drawings of buildings over the silhouettes on the bogus paper. (See Illustration 8-16.) *Note:* Encourage them to use the continuous line drawing on the manila paper as reference.
- Trace over the crayon lines with a black felt marker.
- Dampen the end of the chalk in the water and add small patches of color to a window, step, door, or brick here and there on the composition. *Note:* Lines should not be covered with the chalk color.

*Can You Imagine . . .*

Paste tissue paper building silhouettes on the bogus paper. Make a continuous line drawing of buildings over the tissue using a felt marker.

Cut out pictures of buildings from magazines. Paste them on the bogus paper. Use a waterproof felt marker to draw a continuous line composition of buildings over the cutouts.

Make crayon continuous line drawings of two of Utrillo's prints, one over the other. Add color to the small areas to enhance the composition.

## SYNCRASY (GRADES 5-6)

To create a statement with color, texture, and repetition.

*You'll Need . . .*

Manila paper 6″ × 9″ (2 sheets per child) • crayons (24 colors per box) • at least 2 prints by each of these artists: Gauguin's *Breton Village Under Snow, Riders on the Beach, Tahitian Landscape, Street in Tahiti,* Van Gogh's *Crows Over a Wheat Field, Starry Night, Sidewalk Cafe at Night,* Monet's *Charing Cross Bridge, Cathedral in the Morning, Impres-*

sion Mist, Vase of Chrysanthemums • scissors • cardboard 9″ × 12″ (2 per child) • white glue • No. 12 paintbrushes • jar lids each containing 2 tablespoons of black tempera • pastel colors of construction paper 12″ × 18″ • pastel half sticks of colored chalk (3 pieces per child's choice) • 3″ × 5″ index cards • jar lids each containing 2 tablespoons of water • paper towels (2 per child).

*Procedures . . .*

- Fold the manila paper in half twice vertically and twice horizontally to form 16 spaces.
- Place the paper horizontally on the desk and write with crayon *summer, fall, winter, spring* in the spaces of the first column on the left. (See Illustration 8-17.)

| | | | |
|---|---|---|---|
| summer | | | |
| fall | | | |
| winter | | | |
| spring | | | |

**ILLUSTRATION 8-17**
**CHART FOR**
**SEASONS'**
**COLORS**

- Have children each select three colors of crayon that remind them of summer and color one color in each of the three spaces of the row next to the word *summer. Note:* Encourage them to fill each space completely with color.
- In like manner select colors and color the spaces for *fall, winter,* and *spring*.
- Fold and label the second sheet of manila paper to match the first. *Note:* Do not color the spaces.
- Display the prints and encourage discussion: Which prints contain predominantly warm colors? (See Chapter 2.) How do these warm colors affect the mood of the composition? Does the mood appear quiet, mysterious, or exciting? Which colors make a picture appear cool? (See Chapter 2.) Which season could these colors represent? What mood do these seasonal colors suggest?
- Have children each select a picture that makes them think of summer and decide which three colors dominate the composition.
- Put these three colors in the spaces for summer on the second sheet of paper.
- Repeat the procedure for each of the other seasons. *Note:* Encourage children to analyze the colors and blend colors where necessary to match those in the prints. Children place both sheets of manila paper side by side and compare the colors they themselves used for each season with those that were used in the prints. Ask which colors are similar. Which ones are different? Which group of colors seem to best represent a particular season? Why?

**ILLUSTRATION 8-18
CARDBOARD BUILDING
SHAPES**

- Have children cut one cardboard into several building shapes.
- Cut one or two windows and/or doors in each shape (Illustration 8-18).
- Glue the building shapes on the other piece of cardboard and let them dry.
- Paint the building cutouts with a thick coat of black tempera paint.
- Press the painted surface face down on the construction paper to make a print of the building shapes. (See Illustration 8-19A.) *Note:* Rub the back of the cardboard to get a clearer print. Have children carefully lift the cardboard from the paper.

**ILLUSTRATION 8-19A
SYNCRASY**

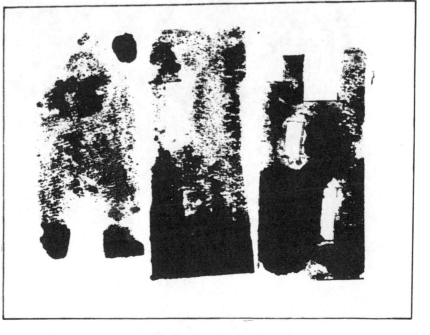

- Paint the building cutouts again with black tempera and make another print of the
buildings on the construction paper, overlapping a part of the previous print. (See

**ILLUSTRATION 8-19B**

**ILLUSTRATION 8-19C**

Illustration 8-19B.) *Note:* Children may print more building shapes on the paper if desired. Then have them place the printing board, the print, and brushes aside.

- Have children select three colors of chalk that could be used on the building composition to suggest a particular season and a mood. *Note:* Encourage children to use the information on the folded manila paper for reference.
- Fold about 1/2″ edges on the index card to form a tray to hold the chalk when not in use.
- Dip the flat end of the chalk in the water and color spaces between the building prints, blending the colors in some areas. *Note:* Children should not color over the tempera paint.
- Cut about a 2″ × 1″ rectangle from a cardboard scrap.
- Dip the edge of the cardboard scrap in the tempera paint and stamp or print accent lines around doors and sides of buildings, or create brick patterns on some buildings. (See Illustration 8-19C.)

### Can You Imagine . . .

Use felt markers to draw other city objects on the composition (such as telephone wires, fire hydrants, signs, billboards).

Use on the building prints crayon and chalk colors that best illustrate one of the following statements: "The city is flashes of color, light, and patterns." "The city is bricks, patterns, and textures." "The city is a maze of form, shape, and patterns." "The city is purple and blue shadows."

Do a thick, heavy, waxed crayon line drawing of various building shapes on 12″ × 18″ drawing paper. Coat the cardboard building shapes with tempera paint and print over the crayon line drawing. Blend pastel colors of chalk on selected areas of the composition.

# INDEX